lopted Children

Adopted Children

Jan de Hartog

Introduction
by
Edmund Blair Bolles

New York   ADAMA BOOKS

Copyright © by Marjorie M. de Hartog and Alan U. Schwartz, Trustees

Reprinted by permission or Atheneum Publishers, Inc.

Library of Congress Cataloging-in-Publication Data

De Hartog, Jan, 1914 –
Adopted children.

Previously published in London in 1969 as: The children.
1. Children, Adopted – Biography. 2. Oriental children – Biography. I. Title.
HV874.8.D4 1987 362.7'34'0924 [B] 87-1846
ISBN 0–915361–65–5 (pbk.)

Printed in Israel

Adama Books, 306 West 38 Street, New York, N.Y. 10018

To Mary L. Graves,
social worker,
on behalf of Hwa Ran, Soo Ja,
Chang Hyang Mi, Nguyen Van Thuan,
Ho Thi Suyet Anh and the hundreds of other
children from Asia who owe her
their life and happiness

INTRODUCTION
by Edmund Blair Bolles

Not long ago I spoke with the director of one of America's most diehard conservative adoption agencies. She described her standards for successful adoption applicants: no working wives, no partners over forty, no previous marriage. The one standard the agency had relaxed concerned the biological mothers. The agency would now place a child for adoption even if, at some time in her life, the mother had smoked marijuana.

The agency worked hard at making the closest match of child and adoptive family, devoting special care to finding physical matches—blue eyes to blue, tall natural to tall adoptive mothers, and so forth. I asked the director why she stressed physical similarity so heavily. The question took her aback. She had never imagined that any other approach might be desirable.

I left that interview with the same sense of dismay I would have felt after emerging from a time capsule. The upheavals of the past years had somehow happened without this woman ever noticing that anything important was underway. Her values and attitude toward adoption had dominated the whole system until the end of the 1960s, but today her agency seems as bizarre a holdover from the past as the municipality of Liechtenstein.

Few practices show the depth of America's recent social changes as starkly as adoption. Ideas about family, individual worth, and hopes for the future all intersect in adoption and all have changed. The old ideas, we can now see, held a shocking contempt for individuality.

The diehard director saw the "best" family in rigid terms that focused on externals. The husband was a good breadwinner; the wife a contented homemaker. Their income and church-going habits commanded respect. Contemporary adoptions are more flexible. Families need not even have a married couple at the head, although usually they do. In judging contemporary adoptions, the emphasis is on the internals. Will a person take a child for better or worse, in sickness and in health? Will the adopter love and respect the child from this day forth? If the answer to these sorts of questions are yes, modern intermediaries are much more willing to pronounce a couple parent and child than the diehard director ever could be.

Contemporary adoptions stress accepting a child on its own terms. Instead of the diehard approach of finding the roundest peg for a pre-cut round hole, adoption intermediaries today urge people to get to know their child. Parents, of course, have much to teach, but they have much to learn as well. They must discover what moves their child. If they stick only to the teaching side, they eventually whistle in the wind. They no longer know what the child needs to learn. The child quits listening. A parent who learns where a child's tastes and talents lie can stay a parent much longer, guiding the child toward the richest and most humane part of his nature.

In 1968, however, the diehard director was no diehard, but a typical proponent of agency values. In that year Jan de Hartog published his book about the adoption of children from Asia. To agency people, the book surely seemed as strange as the diehard director seemed to me. To the adoption experts of 1968 Mr. de Hartog's book was also a step into a time machine, only one that went forward. He expressed the values and assumptions of adoptions in the 1980s. After a long period out of print, 1987 is the perfect time to republish it.

Mr. de Hartog has given us something special. Personal accounts of one family's experience with adoption are commonplace and seldom worth preserving. But de Hartog has given us a pearl of great price. I might even call it a classic, if I didn't suspect the word would frighten off some readers. In school a classic was a dull book of noble purpose. Mr de Hartog's book is never dull. It is a work created in an earlier age that still speaks to us with a freshness and immediacy that more recent books cannot dampen. He writes with a vitality and honesty that brings the subject home to the reader.

The book is practical, and yet it says almost nothing about how to adopt. Just as well, however, for almost everything in that regard has changed since the book was published. In those days you approached an agency. If the agency turned you down, you went home and bought a cat. Today agencies play a less dominating role. There are also parent groups and child advocacy groups to provide information, and there are several types of adoption intermediaries. Anyone beginning to adopt today should survey their local situation carefully to learn the best information. Never assume that your local adoption agency is the only story, or even that it knows the whole story.

Mr. de Hartog assumes that you have adopted a child and then offers practical advice about what sorts of problems arise and what to do about them. De Hartog writes about adopting Asian children. Since he wrote, America has seen a growth in adoptions from Asia, Latin America, and the United States' own tragically large pool of waiting children. Almost everything Mr. de Hartog writes applies equally to these new adoptions. The problems he addresses probably struck the typical agency director of twenty years ago as rare and peculiar. Today they are the commonplaces of adoption talk. But although experts now recognize the problems, de Hartog's loving and unsentimental approach is as fresh as good milk.

De Hartog's honesty shines through his prose. I have read more personal accounts of adoption than I care to count, but most do not merit much attention. They are honorable, but too easily impressed with their own emotions. It is more fun to think, "wow, I can love and feel," than it is to read somebody else think it. Mr. de Hartog won my trust early, when I read his sentence, "Although I am just as self-centered as I was twenty years ago, somehow my concept of self has expanded." Love, not sentiment, is the basis of adoption, and when I read that sentence I knew de Hartog could talk straight about building on love.

The book's universality comes from interweaving its two enduring themes. One is the parent-child relationship, a natural part of any adoption story. The other theme is less obvious but just as important: courtship. Normally, we speak of courtship between two adults thinking about marriage. Each has to learn the other's ways and discover respect for qualities in the other that the self never developed. In Mr. de Hartog's discussion of adoptions, the courtship is between adult and child. It is an old-fashioned courtship with honorable intentions declared at the outset, but the courtship questions still dominate: How can you be this way? How can I tolerate that? Must I do all the accepting and understanding? Only instead of winning a spouse, the courtier woos a child. Mr. de Hartog has given us a practical book full of concrete truths about how to court a child so that the pair of you form a family.

Every classic, however, includes some elements from its own age that readers must make allowances for. In Mr. de Hartog's case, the only seriously dated part of his voice comes from his complete lack of anticipation of the women's movement that has swept through America. I don't mean that de Hartog patronizes women. He does not. When he speaks of women and adoption he refers to their role as mothers, and, of course that role persists but de Hartog never implies that motherhood defines the whole range of a woman's potential. Instead, he patronizes men. His is the voice of an age when the image of a man rocking a baby was always good for a laugh in TV comedy. In those days the idea of a loving father acting sensitively toward an unhappy child seem intrinsically absurd. De Hartog knew himself well enough to know that he loved children and that his love was good, but he was enough of a part of his own time to patronize himself as an awkward male. My advice for when you read these passages of female chauvinism is to blush a little for what we once were, and keep on reading. This is a splendid book.

Contents

One: The Beginning

Two: Settling Down

Three: Family Life

Appendices

Preface to First Edition

AT PRESENT, the majority of Asian orphans coming to the United States for adoption are children of mixed parentage from Korea. A small number come from Hong Kong; an even smaller one, thus far, from Vietnam.

By now, over ten thousand children from Korea have become part of American families. Most of these children are the issue of common-law relationships between Korean girls from the provinces and American servicemen. Often the parents have gone through a wedding ceremony in one of the "marriage offices" set up for this purpose in Korean cities by unscrupulous businessmen; the girl may not be aware of the fact that the procedure has no legal validity, the father certainly is. He proceeds to set up house with her and, eventually, there are children. As a rule, the termination of his service in Korea puts an end to the relationship; only in rare cases does he show any further interest in his Korean family. He may send money for a while, but this soon ceases; after that there is nothing but silence; as far as the father is concerned the episode is closed. Without its operatic trappings, the story of Madame Butterfly is re-enacted in

Korea hundreds of times each year. Most Americans, if they are aware of the existence of these children at all, assume the emergency to be over, as the war ended fifteen years ago; but there are still sixty thousand U.S. servicemen stationed in Korea and many families are still being abandoned, with all that this entails in the way of heartbreak and tragedy.

To begin with, the mother, left to feed and clothe and educate the child after the man she supposed to be her husband has left her, is ostracized by her family because her child is not only of mixed race but also, it now turns out, illegitimate. Korean family structure is very clannish and moral traditions are severe; in that paternal society, where women do not count for much anyhow, the ones who transgress, be it unknowingly, are cast out without compunction. Their children, who by their very appearance carry a stigma, face an even harder time. Their pure-blood playmates discriminate against them and physically abuse them at every opportunity. They are chased, cornered, beaten, stoned; their hair is pulled out, their clothes are torn. School is out of the question; their only hope for an education is in small private classes where the teaching is haphazard at best. The mother has no means of earning a livelihood; unless her family relents, or she places her child for adoption overseas, she has no alternative but to become a camp-follower. This decision is further influenced by the fact that in the so-called "recreation villages" that have proliferated along the 38th parallel children of mixed race are in the majority. Although the atmosphere of these villages can hardly be considered suitable for a growing child, there at least he is free from persecution and harassment by his contemporaries.

Some Korean girls, especially those from the sheltered world of well-to-do families, cannot face this prospect and will get rid of their children by any means. Newborn babies are frequently drowned in the river or left on the steps of churches or temples. The infants who survive are put in orphanages, where the same ostracism and contempt await them that they would have faced in the world outside.

Children of mixed parentage have no future in Korea. Although recently a first effort has been made by the Korean government to provide them with jobs, so far the male offspring of American servicemen will be able to earn a living only in the underworld, by crime or procuring; for girls of mixed blood there is no future except in the recreation villages.

The U.S. military and government show an unbecoming callousness toward these children, having refused to undertake any responsibility for them. It is left to "private enterprise" to ease their lot, and a few organizations have tried to do so. Shortly after the war the writer Pearl Buck arranged for a number of these children to be brought to the United States through "Welcome House," an adoption agency specializing in the placement of Asian children which she founded twenty years ago. An Oregon farmer named Harry Holt, with no help except from members of his family, founded an orphanage in South Korea, placed over four thousand children of mixed race with families in the United States and adopted eight of them himself. His methods for the placement of children were desperate in a desperate situation; welfare agencies and professional social workers considered them irresponsible and prevailed upon Congress to pass a law curtailing his activities, which brought about his death from a heart attack soon thereafter. His name survives in an agency that still places Korean children for adoption.

The number of children coming to the U.S. from Hong Kong, usually full Chinese and selected from the hundreds of abandoned urchins that used to roam the city in packs, has been reduced of late owing to local relief programs. As to Vietnam, besides the children actually orphaned by the war, during the past few years more and more have been abandoned in some chaotic exodus after the civilian population of a hamlet or town was bombed or forced to evacuate at a moment's notice, usually at dead of night. As a result, a number of children in the overcrowded and pitiful orphanages of Saigon and in the countryside are not orphaned at all, but simply separated from their parents; the presence of these children is, for the time being, one of the main reasons for the U.S. government's objection to the placement of any Vietnamese orphans for adoption overseas. Conscientious social workers in key positions balk at the idea that a child sent abroad for placement may have óne or both parents living somewhere in the chaos of South Vietnam; to call a child an orphan before a thorough investigation has become possible constitutes to them a violation of their professional ethics, even if many children, especially infants, are doomed to die within a matter of months if they remain where they are. In Appendix A to this book a report can be found on conditions in these orphanages as I came to know them through personal experience. In the summer of 1966 my wife and I became part of a Quaker "Meeting for Sufferings," formed with the intention of helping the children of Vietnam. One of its objectives was to place foundlings for adoption with families overseas—the only solution in their case, as infant mortality was at that time officially estimated at between fifty and seventy percent, depending on the orphanage.

In the process we ourselves became the adoptive parents of two Korean girls, now aged five and seven. When they came to us, we felt the urgent need for advice and reassurance from someone with experience. We were fortunate in that among our neighbors there was a family with five children, three of them from Korea; without the help and guidance of Grace and Stanford Kight of Concordville, Pennsylvania, we would have had a difficult time indeed.

A few days after the children's arrival in our home, we were interviewed on Dutch television, and a photograph of our family with its new additions was shown on the screen. The surprising result was that nearly a thousand families in Holland applied for a similar child; the first reaction of the authorities was a blank refusal to let any Asian children into the country. As a result of public pressure, however, the Minister of Justice appointed a commission "to study the advisability of interracial adoptions in the Netherlands." It was the commission's initial contention that these adoptions were, as a rule, much less likely to "succeed" than normal ones; but this was indeed no more than a contention, as interracial adoptions had been virtually unknown in Holland until then. To help the commission on its deliberations I prevailed upon over a hundred adoptive parents, in this country belonging to the "Welcome House Adoptive Parents Group," to write down their experiences with their children; their letters were forwarded to the Netherlands and resulted in a more lenient attitude; ultimately, 450 children were admitted for adoption.

The fact that their parents would have no one to turn to for advice prompted me to write this collection of random notes on the practical aspects of interracial adoption, based on my own experiences and those of the parents who wrote the letters. I concern myself mainly with the child over the age of three not only because our own children were in this age group when they arrived, but because babies are likely to adapt much more readily and the number of subjects on which specialized advice will be needed is limited in their case.

I do not pretend to have covered all problems, large and small, that the adoptive parent of an Asian child is likely to encounter. I do not claim any professional authority either, other than that of a battle-scarred father of six. But I did correspond with a large number of fellow adoptive parents of Asian children, and we agreed that this was the type of information we would have liked to have.

At times, while reading this book, you may suddenly become aware of the fact that most of the problems, joys and conflicts of parenthood are described as seen from the mother's point of view. As the father is, normally, away during the daytime, the main part of the burden of helping the child adjust to its new surroundings rests on the shoulders of the mother. As a writer, and thus an incurable ham, I could not help putting myself in her place to an extent that may on occasion give cause to psychoanalytical musings on the part of the reader. I remember what my first reaction was when I heard, some years ago, my wife's gynecologist exclaim, "I *honestly* don't think any man can truly know what we girls go through during pregnancy!" As he was, in private life, a cigar-chomping baseball fan with a family of eight, I took his startling identification with his patients as an innocent occupational aberration; I trust the reader will, in my case, conclude the same.

During the writing, when it became obvious that I would have to reveal a number of personal things about Eva and Julia de Hartog, my wife and I had many discussions as to whether this would constitute an invasion of their privacy. We finally decided that the help our children might thus give to their less fortunate contemporaries outweighed all other considerations. For my hope is that this book may encourage couples who are thinking of adoption to consider adopting a child from Asia and, should they decide to do so, to take an older one. Any child over the age of three is officially considered "hard to place"; large numbers of them, here as well as abroad, have little hope of ever realizing their full potential unless they find parents who will encourage and stimulate them with interest and affection.

To those among us who are concerned about the future, this clearly presents an area worthy of consideration. For although their number may be "like that of the sands of the sea," as one brochure on the plight of the mixed-race children of Korea put it, this much we know: each one of these children, individually, is of infinite value to mankind.

J. *de* H.

One

The Beginning

1

The Decision

By the time you arrive at your decision to adopt a child from Asia, you will have heard many objections and warnings. Some of these are dealt with in Appendix A to this book; when all is said and done, there will be one crucial question left for you to face. If you are young, with small children of your own, you will ask yourself, "How will it affect them?" If you are in the age group of those whose children have flown the coop, you will ask, "Am I too old?"

In the first case, your children will be delighted at the prospect of having a little brother or sister from Vietnam or Korea. As a matter of fact, you had better go easy here; once you mention the possibility, they may not leave you in peace until you have made it a fact. To young children the idea of a brother from China (this is, for some reason, children's general term for the Far East) is full of romantic excitement. They see themselves

3

showing him off to their classmates and their friends, pro-
tecting him against bullies, stalking with him through the
forest, where he will lead them, sniffing the ground on
hands and knees, to the lair of the fox or—who knows?
—the mountain lion. I know of a little boy who, when told
that a little sister was born, burst into tears and sobbed,
"I had so hoped it would be a little elephant." This is not
just a funny story; up to the age of, say, five, a child's
world is made up of people and animals in equal proportions, all of whom have full human rights. The dog is as
much of a person to him as Aunt Frances, maybe even
more so; "a little elephant" and "a little Chinese" are not
so different from each other as you might hope after all
those sessions in Sunday School. Your problem will be to
get the little Chinese out of the little-elephant stage into
the reality of a competitor for your children's toys, their
playroom, your attention and, above all, your affection.
There is one instance where a happy but immature family with three spoiled little boys committed the folly of
applying not only for one, but for two children from
Asia. The social worker who studied the home must have
had her doubts, but as the family was, outwardly at least,
kind, well-integrated and affluent, there was no valid reason for not letting two orphaned siblings profit from this
rare opportunity. The two children came; after the
shortest of honeymoons, the three little boys were so
overcome by jealousy that they literally drove the inter-
lopers out of the house. They beat them, kicked them,
rode into them with their tricycles; the whole thing became such a barroom fight that the Asian children had to
be removed in a hurry. What this did to the emotional
balance of the two orphans, who during the six months

before their arrival must have idealized their future family out of all proportion, can be imagined.

Obviously, you should do everything in your power to prevent this elementary mistake. There are a few pointers that will indicate whether your decision to adopt a child from Asia may lead to serious trouble with your children. Have you decided to adopt one because you want a playmate for your own child? Experienced social workers, the moment they hear a parent say, "Oh, our Lucy is so lonely, she badly needs a little companion," will discourage adoption. Or do you—and your children, for that matter—think of the adoption of the new Asian brother or sister as a rescue operation? "We are adopting a dear little boy who otherwise would end up as a little beggar." In that case it is almost inevitable that you will at a given moment in the future turn around and demand gratitude from the waif you saved. We all fondly believe that the days of slavery are over, but to have an adopted child whom you expect to be grateful is not so far removed from *Uncle Tom's Cabin* as you may think. The humane impulse is as valid and sound a motive for adoption as infertility, but it requires sober scrutiny on your part.

You might as well face it: once you introduce any little brother or sister into your family, there are, after a short period of euphoria, bound to be conflicts that show a side of your children's character with which you will be less than delighted. The newcomer in his turn may prove to be as tough and hard-bitten in the battle of survival in the playroom as he was in the alleys of Saigon or Seoul. Conflicts are unavoidable even when a new child is born into a family; they are compounded and fraught with potential ugliness when the child is an orphan from overseas.

But once the conflicts are behind you, there can be no doubt that your family life will be immensely enriched. I know several families where natural and adopted Asian children are mixed; they are among the happiest of my acquaintance even though sometimes the walls seem to be torn asunder by rows like eruptions of Mount Krakatau. Most Korean boys especially are made of tough stuff indeed; one parent compared them to the Sabras of Israel: the generation that was born there and grew up in the tumultuous period, full of danger, that marked the rebirth of the nation. I mention this because it would be wrong to picture these children in your mind as cowering, frightened little urchins who will shrink at every sight and start at every sound. They are, in most cases, the battle-scarred veterans of a bitter struggle for survival and it is, almost without exception, only the toughest and brightest who make it. So do not think that when a fight erupts it must always be the fault of your own children; at times it may be they who need protection, not the sad, delicate little creature with the huge black eyes.

The only way to forestall serious trouble is to talk the adoption over thoroughly with your children before you undertake any steps in that direction. Make sure they understand that they are not going to receive a little playmate but a competitor, and that the child when he finally arrives is probably going to be hard to live with, at least for a while. Even though this may seem unrealistic in view of their age, impress upon them that they share the responsibility for your decision, should you decide to go ahead. Then, when the inevitable conflagration comes, they cannot turn around and hold you uniquely responsible for foisting on them a cuckoo that is now trying to push them out of the nest. And when the battle comes, do not take it too seriously; children fight without any delicacy and without adhering to any rules, but somehow these fights do not destroy their sense of kinship, they rather tend to increase it. Our two little daughters fight at times so furiously that to us the rift seems permanent. They will tell us they hate each other, that Eva is mean or Julie is stupid and that they will never speak to each other again; five minutes later they will be squealing with delight as one rolls the other down the garden path in a plastic wastebasket—for which they are reprimanded, as it belongs in Daddy's study. A reprimand welds them into a tight little unit of sisterly love and makes them behave, for the next ten minutes at least, like Siamese twins.

There are in America a good many families of which Korean orphans have been part for sixteen years or more. Their verdict is unanimous: it may take time, but in the end the child from Asia is completely accepted as a member of the family; after a few years it will seem incredible that he was not born into it.

Will the child himself, at times, feel like an outsider, even though your own children accept him completely as a brother? Certainly. He may even, when an order or a refusal has aroused his resentment, say that he wants to go back to Korea. This will alarm you, until you have the same experience as a good friend of ours who has one Korean daughter and one of her own. When her natural daughter was told one night that she could not stay up to see Lassie on television, she said, "I'm sick of this! I'm

going back to Korea!" Maybe this will help you to keep
your cool when the straw fires of childhood fury rage
around you and smoke gets in your eyes.

As to those among you who ask yourselves: "Aren't we
too old to adopt a child?" I can sympathize with them; as
I write this, I am fifty-three years old and my younger
daughter is four. The first comment I can offer is that
Dutch law, notoriously ungenerous when it comes to
adoptions, allows a parent to be fifty years older than his
or her youngest adoptive child. If the dour and uncompromising Calvinists of yore, whose sole objective was to
make adoption as difficult as possible, permitted a man to
be fifty years older than his youngest child, there should
be no need for any of us to worry. I am in a position to
expand a little on this, for apart from my adopted daughters I have four grown-up children and two grandchil-
dren. This should, to all intents and purposes, make me
feel like a senior citizen; and occasionally it does. But
when I leaf through diaries I occasionally kept in the past,
I am struck by the discovery that I felt like a senior citizen at times when, from where I now stand, I was a dash-
ing spring cockerel. I wrote a book once called *A Sailor's
Life*, containing a series of small essays on ships and the
sea; many of the letters I received from its readers seemed
to suggest that they visualized me as an ancient mariner,
complete with rubber-tipped cane and wispy white
beard, gazing nostalgically out over the sea that had once
been his life. At the time I wrote it I was barely forty
years old, a mere snotnose compared to the irascible old
salt I consider myself to be nowadays.

Some of our worry makes sense, however. A man gets
older; it slows down his reactions, at least his physical

ones, and it makes him a little more staid in his actions and his thinking. But to young children this is an advantage rather than a drawback in a father. I may not burst forth yodeling from my bedroom after three hour's healthy sleep, to slap my buttocks and bellow in the shower; nobody, not even a child of four takes kindly to this narcissistic virility at the crack of dawn. I may not put them both on my back and race about the house on hands and knees as fathers do in advertisements for carpeting or air-conditioners; I chase them occasionally, oblige with a spine-tingling "Boo!" from a wardrobe and promptly collapse in my easy chair, where I sit panting for the next quarter hour, fanning myself with *Parents' Magazine.* I may be less eager to go for nature rambles or gritty picnics on distant beaches, I have a lot more patience with small children than I used to in my zestier years. For one thing, although I am just as self-centered as I was twenty years ago, somehow my concept of self has expanded. Whereas in the past I used to roam through my house and family like a tight little island full of individual dreams, plans, secret joys and sorrows, bent on defending my independence ruthlessly, I now seem to include my family in my concept of self. I defend that self as determinedly against outside interference as I once defended my smaller ego, but within its magic circle I am just as interested in the thoughts, dreams, joys and sorrows of my children as I once was in my own. Twenty-five years ago, children were noisy, smelly table-bangers in fierce competition with myself for the attention of their mother. They seemed obsessed by some spiteful demon which prompted them to burst into the living room bawling, diapers oozing, just as I was reading the day's work to some enraptured friends; whenever they had a running cold, their first reaction was to make a bee-line for me and sneeze snottily in my face, so that a few nights later, in my lecture to the Literary Society of Rotterdam, I would refer to the poet Johannes Roseman as Johaddes Rosebud. I cannot truthfully say that in those days there was a sacred tie of love between me and my offspring; it seems unfair, but now I not only accept these aspects of fatherhood with good grace, I positively dote on the two little beasts who so suddenly burst upon me in my dotage.

Just as the worry about growing old is a young man's worry, to feel younger than ever is an old man's delusion. Even so, I honestly have never for a single moment felt "old" in connection with my two youngest children. This did not come as a surprise to me; my own father was forty-eight when I was born, yet I never thought of him as an old man. That is to say, I thought him just as ancient, crotchety, cantankerous and barnacle-encrusted as my contemporaries judged their fathers to be who were twenty years younger, but I had a much more intimate relationship with my father than most other boys had with theirs. He used to listen to me, for one thing, and not with the insufferably superior smile of an adult indulging Junior, but with genuine interest. There were times, later, when I suspected that all he had been, in truth, was a better actor than those younger fathers, but now I know from my own experience that his interest was genuine. He must have been truly fascinated by my stories about two monkeys who escaped from the zoo, stole a rowboat and started a career as porthole builders, which necessitated their sawing round holes in the flanks of ships at night in order to drum up some business. He must have been just as spellbound by this juvenile fantasy, its inventiveness and intricate ramifications, as I am by my youngest daughter's rambling saga of a family of mice who try to wake her up at night to make her play with them and who, when she refuses because they can sleep all day while she has to go to school, sit down at the playroom table and swap stories while Mother Mouse makes little capes for them out of Kleenex, which look cute but show their bottoms. I wouldn't swap that story for any of the mechanical drivel I am invited to read in today's magazines.

To sum up: if I had to choose, at the age of four, between Marlon Brando for a father or Jimmy Durante, guess whom I would select. And, frankly, wouldn't you?

2

The First Steps

You have made your decision, contacted one of the agencies specializing in the placement of Oriental children (see Appendix C), and probably attended a group meeting during which the director of the agency explained its work, procedures and "guidelines." If the guidelines have not ruled you out, you can now at any moment expect a visit from the social worker in charge of your case, who will do your home-study.

Adoptive parents, especially adoptive mothers, are supposed to loathe their caseworkers with the same intensity and impulsiveness with which natural mothers adore their obstetricians. Usually the reasons for this phenomenon cannot be laid at the door of the worker but are inherent in the situation. While a natural conception and pregnancy are about the most intimate experiences a woman can go through, the process of adoption will make her feel as if her deepest secrets were being spread about in a succession of impersonal documents, in triplicate.

Confronted by a person who doesn't know her from Eve but is about to rule on whether she shall have a child or no, any woman's natural reaction is, "Who the hell does she think she is?" Most people, out of fear of the caseworker who is to rule on whether or not they get a child, put up with her and her searching questions as a necessary evil rather than as someone who might profitably be listened to in the process of their self-evaluation. In the nature of things, she is the defender of the child against the impetuosity, ignorance or emotional immaturity of his prospective adoptive parents. She may occasionally give you the impression that you are guilty unless proven innocent and that all she is interested in is what you are hiding from her; the older and more experienced the social worker, the more relaxed and informal she will be. The best ones among them have developed an unerring intuition; their judgment of the suitability of parents has little to do with the book any more and is based almost entirely on experience. I'll never forget how surprised and put out we were when the social worker who studied our home did not betray the slightest interest in the children's rooms Marjorie had so carefully prepared for her inspection, but brushed the suggestion aside with the words, "I didn't suppose you'd stick 'em in the cellar." She professed a case-hardened toughness, yet to see this woman with a child was an unforgettable experience; neither before nor since have I met anyone in whom tenderness and compassion blended so homogeneously with common sense.

So, do not give in too readily to your instinctive distrust of the woman who comes to ask you, with a clipboard on her knee, why you are infertile, how long you and your husband have tried to effect natural impregnation, why you have now decided you want somebody else's child, and why you state as your preference a child from Asia. Read back to you like that, your own statements may sound distressing; the reason for your insistence on adopting an orphan half a world away will take some explaining, because she has in her files four orphans in your own community for whom she has been unable to find suitable homes. To her, every child in her files is a live, real, suffering human being whereas yours will be a faceless case from some Asian social worker's files that she is requested to place without any hope for reciprocity. She will study you on the sober consideration that it is better to place some needy child than none at all; but you may have a hard time convincing her that you haven't chosen an Asian child the way you might choose a fur coat or an automobile: as a status symbol or as the result of a current fad.

Of course there are high-handed, insensitive and pompous social workers because, like ourselves, they belong to the human race, but I have never met one in connection with the actual placement of a child. Those I did meet were usually at the top of the bureaucratic hierarchy, in governments or large charitable organizations. The reason for their preference of procedures over people was usually not that they were cruel or callous by nature, but simply that they had not set eyes on a living child for years, sometimes decades; what they were shuffling on their desks was children's records. I suspect that even I, who think of myself in such laudatory terms of humanity and compassion, would find it hard to visualize a tear-streaked little face or discern a forlorn cry among those mountains of manila envelopes, each containing, in dreary multinumbered forms, a human fate, an inexorable destiny, in which I would be involved only in a purely mechanical way, like a guillotine.

Once your home-study is made and you have been accepted, the process known as "matching" begins. Most agencies will be at pains to keep up the fiction that it is you who choose the child and not they; in practice this is rarely the case. Even if they have a bulletin board with the photographs of available children, it is not customary that you stand in front of it and "pick the best of the litter," as one director of Wagnerian dimensions once put it to me. The agency, after the home-study, has a definite opinion as to what type of child will be most congenial to you and your family; they will select a child on the basis of the information at their disposal.

In the case of local children, this information is extensive, at least on the parents of the child. Agencies are great believers in heredity; if a child is the offspring of two parents with high IQ's, it is assumed that he will be more intelligent than most; if the father was an athlete, a boy will be described as "sturdy" or "muscular"; if the mother is pretty, her baby girl will be "a beautiful child" although during the first weeks of their existence the human young present a fairly uniform and generally unprepossessing appearance. Fanciful as some of these descriptions may be, at least they give the prospective adoptive parents something to read to appease their hunger for information on their future child.

In Asia, where the children are studied by local social workers, certain stereotyped ideas appear to be prevalent

as to what American parents are looking for. Baby girls
will be referred to as "cute," "dimpled," "lively" and
"normal for their age," while in cases of mixed parentage the caseworker will be looking for characteristics of
the father's race rather than the mother's. An American-
Korean baby is likely to have "large, Caucasian-shaped
eyes," "dark brown hair" rather than black, while curls
and waves are reported with enthusiasm. The photograph
that accompanies the descriptions is usually a snapshot
made by the social worker herself, or by the director of
the reception center or the orphanage; in my experience,
only one reception center felt moved to cut off that most
depressing detail of orphans' photographs, the serial number. To us the spectacle of a shy, appealing little girl of
two gazing at the camera with a mixture of alarm and fas-
cination while holding in front of her stomach a slate
with the number 23896–F is likely to be painful, at least
at first sight. In the case of babies, the snapshot, taken in
a police post when the child was brought in as a foundling
or in a temporary foster home, will rarely be properly focused; after having been Xeroxed three or four times it
may be cause for nervous little jokes between the future
parents, like "Well, darling, it seems we are adopting the
Dalai Lama." But in a matter of days the blurred snapshot
will begin to undergo a magical change. Gradually, it will
reveal details and characteristics that in the end will add
up to a complete picture of the child they now expect. I
might as well save myself the trouble of trying to prevail
upon you not to take that first photograph too seriously,
it is unavoidable that you will. The picture will end up by
acquiring a personality of its own, not as the image of a
distant human being, but in its own right. I am familiar

with that situation; when I was a young sailor, after a voyage of fourteen months the photograph of my girl-friend in my bunk would have turned into the real thing and the girl herself into its unsatisfactory imitation. Like my girlfriend, your child in the flesh will turn out to be quite different from the snapshot, and not just outwardly. For one thing, it was taken six months earlier, and six months is a long time in the life of a small child; also, it shows only one of the surprising variety of expressions even the youngest face can display. It depends entirely on the moment when the shutter clicked whether you will be led to expect a gay, a solemn, a puckish or a calmly de-termined child.

You are not the only one involved in this first photo-graphic encounter: your child too is given photographs and a description of his future parents, and most likely their effect on him will be stronger than that of his snap-shot on you. The agency may ask you for a series of photographs, in color: one of each of you alone; one of the two of you on a couch where there is room for more; if you have a family, your children will be photographed separately and not in your company. I must warn you against photographing pets; in principle the presence of a shaggy dog or a snuggly cat would seem to be a reassur-ing item to a child; pets, however, may die or run away between the time the photograph is made and the arrival of the child. The first thing he will do is to rush into the house and ask for the dog or the cat; if you fail to pro-duce either one, it will not only be a bitter disappoint-ment to him but add to his sense of insecurity. But you should include snapshots of your house and, if you can, of the room and bed where your child will sleep. It is most important that once you have photographed these things, you change them as little as possible; I don't think any of us can know how intensely the children will study these photographs, time and time again, until every particle has become as familiar in their minds as the reality that surrounds them.

At the risk of stampeding you at this delicate juncture, there is a point I feel I should raise. Especially if your child is older than three, he is almost sure to have one or more siblings unmentioned in his case history. Some agencies over there will mention additional children more readily than others, but all of them know from experience that two children are much more difficult to place than one, so more often than not the two are split up and presented separately.

As the father of two little sisters myself, my advice would be to find out whether there are any brothers or sisters belonging to the child allotted to you. If so, consider seriously whether you might not be able to take in two instead of one. After comparing notes with other families I have come to the conclusion that, on the whole, the taking in of two children has a tendency to solve more problems than it creates. For one thing, they help each other to bridge the traumatic gap between the old world and the new. Instead of facing all alone an entirely new and alien reality without any vestige left from the old, the two siblings will face the transition together; to each of them the other will be an all-important link with the past. Also, two children tend to keep each other busy; they play together, have their bath together, go to bed together; it is amazing how much sheer drudgery a second child takes over from the mother.

But the main reason for keeping brothers and sisters together is that, once they are permanently split up, they will never cease to grieve for each other. These feelings will rarely come to the surface in the early stages of the adoption; but many parents have told me that, had they only known sooner how much the little brother or sister meant to the child they adopted, they would have taken the other one in without hesitation.

Should you hesitate because you fear that together they will tend to keep you out of their relationship, I can assure you that this will not be the case. There may be times when you will have the feeling that they are ganging up on you, especially when sharing the pleasant fear following a joint transgression, but in reality they will compete for your affection rather than find it between themselves. The relationship between siblings is fundamentally different from that between parent and child; it can only enrich a child and increase his sense of belonging if, apart from a father and a mother, he has a brother or a sister with whom he can share the adventure of childhood.

3

"Pre-adoptive Pregnancy"

THIS is a term some agencies use which may sound as infuriating to you mothers as their term "Paps" for "preadoptive parents" does to us fathers. Yet it is an accurate definition of the state of mind in which the mother will find herself during the months preceding the arrival of her child.

Experts disagree on its ideal duration; some agencies even arrange matters so that the waiting period will conform to their concept of how long it should last. If you adopt a child from Korea or Vietnam, there will be an interval of at least six months anyhow between your filing the application and the day when the plane touches down on the runway, your knees turn to jelly and your eyes fill with idiotic tears as you breathlessly rush to the gate the moment its number is announced. By that time, although you may not be aware of it yourself, a fundamental change has taken place in your connection with the child who is about to be put into your arms. The change is expressed in an unobtrusive transition between your thinking of him as "the child" at first and "my child" later.

The change is indeed like a pregnancy; you will find to your embarrassment that you are showing exactly the same symptoms of mood and behavior. Hours of idle dreaming; total and constant preoccupation with the little life now so tenuously and mysteriously joined with your own; fluctuations between elation and dejection, triggered by preposterously small causes: a casual word, a tune caught on the radio, a headline in a paper, the frown of a stranger in the supermarket. Your mood will turn on a hair and vacillate wildly, leaving you limp, or trembling with an inexplicable nervousness. There will be times when you feel wonderfully secure in your home, your husband's love, your friends, the budding trees in the garden, the sparrows on the windowsill, the dog wagging his tail, the cat stretching his limbs and sharpening his claws on the back of your husband's chair; it all seems to exude a warm, infinitely precious feeling of serenity and joy. At other times, exactly the same things will turn into dark and menacing portents of disaster. Your home is unsuitable for children; your husband's love, which, as we all know, has to be nurtured daily like an expensive plant, will draw away because you seem, to him, to center your entire affection on the child. Your friends will disapprove and make the child feel unwanted; he will climb the tree in the garden when you are not looking, fall out and break his neck; he will, after watching the sparrows peck at the seeds on the windowsill for a while, feel like doing the same and stick their droppings in his mouth, which will give him psittacosis, or whatever the name is of the exotic bird's disease that makes people die screaming.

And this is not all. Your opinion of yourself will be subject to the same vacillations. One day, looking at yourself in the mirror, you feel that this is really what you were created for, that you would like not one, but four, six children; you smile as you look at yourself, for you are looking at a true mother, brimming over with love, calm and competence. The next day, the haggard creature in the mirror will be a barren, neurotic female who in a moment of megalomania and frustration has plunged headlong into a commitment for life to a total stranger, a sinister little foundling who may, for all you know, turn out to be another Jack the Ripper, or merely a juvenile delinquent. What in the name of God made you presume that you had any talent, any natural aptitude for rearing a child of Asian parents and turning it into an All-American football player heading for an executive's office on Madison Avenue, or a pianist performing in Lincoln Center to the thunderous applause of a cheering crowd? So far, your husband has loved you because you have, by the grace of God, been well rested and well balanced enough to hide from him the hissing snake-pit of your true nature. Now, with the arrival of the child, you will, stricken by frenzy, exhausted by insomnia, debilitated by a sense of doom and failure, be unable to keep the lid on your true, dark self and you will have no one to blame for it but yourself, you have brought this catastrophe down on your own head, in a moment of lunacy and self-indulgence. If, in the black, weightless panic of your hysterical dejection, you were to confess all this to your husband in one awful, sobbing explosion, he would turn out to be a dear but useless nincompoop who would know nothing better to do than to smile at your frenzy, pat your shoulder as if you were a horse and try to sell you the snake-pit of your secret vices as a harmless little terrarium.

When the first ripple of the incoming tide of your pre-adoptive pregnancy gives you a faint shiver of inexplicable apprehension, there are several things you can do. To start with, read up on the hints and rules for expectant mothers, which you can get free of charge from the nearest pre-natal clinic, and follow their advice, including vitamins. Then, as soon as possible, seek out other mothers expecting an Asian child, although you may have some difficulty getting their names and addresses out of your agency. For reasons known only to themselves, some agencies do not approve of their Paps getting together. If you are lucky enough to have in your neighborhood a couple who have already adopted children from Korea or Vietnam, go and visit with them. You will find that, despite her frenzied schedule, the mother likes nothing better than to take time off to tell you exactly how she felt when she was in your situation. Then start preparing for your child's arrival.

Those whose profession it is to know about these things say that "mental preparation" is more important than merely building the nest. You may find it difficult, however, to sit down at eleven every morning and devote an hour to mental preparation. The moment you sit down with the intention of concentrating on the spiritual and emotional aspects of the imminent change in your life, your mind will start wandering the way it does in church. You intended to think about Love, Responsibility, the things you will have to Sacrifice, but there you sit: eyes closed, looking like a deeply religious person in earnest meditation, thinking whether it wouldn't be better to go in for a washer-dryer than to use the diaper service, whose truck you have seen drive past with the faintly nauseating name "Wee Moderns."

Don't worry, you will become mentally prepared in direct proportion to the material preparations you undertake. It is impossible to wander through the Baby and Playroom Furniture section of your department store and look at high chairs, playpens and cots in various sizes without visualizing your child in each one of them. While buying his clothes, furnishing the room you have set aside for him, selecting storybook stencils to put on the walls, considering whether, as someone suggested, to hang live goldfish in a water-filled plastic bag inside a baby's crib is a good idea, you are in actual fact making the child more and more real to you. This, as far as I have been able to make out, is what is meant by mental preparation.

A fact you might as well be aware of at this stage is that children from Vietnam and to a certain degree also those from Korea have no idea what toys are. They have certainly never been given the opportunity to familiarize themselves with dolls; so don't, if your child is under three, buy the cutest doll you can find. It will open and shut huge glass eyes, sightless and fixed like those of a blind person; it will squeal "Mommy" when put on its back, a sound no Asian child will associate with motherhood; and if it is one of those that realistically wet their diapers you are truly in for trouble.

Your safest bet is a small, stuffed pussy cat, on condition its eyes are not too realistic and it does not squeak when pressed. Teddy bears are unfamiliar and thus the reverse of reassuring; mechanical toys are not only unfamiliar but too angular to be hugged for comfort.

Believe it or not, when your child is three years old or more, a two-foot length of colored yarn with its ends knotted together will probably give him the most satisfaction. Whether he is from Korea, Vietnam, England, Holland or America, he will instantly know what to do with it: cat's cradles. This is, to me, about the most meaningless game imaginable, as all you can do with a cat's cradle is to let it slip and start all over again; but children judge their games by different standards. Another gift that will instantly be picked up is a toy trumpet, but you may regret that choice when he starts blowing it at dead of night to assert his identity in an unfamiliar and menacing world.

Something you may think of yourself is to be sure to put up a toothbrush holder, a towel rack and a ring for a plastic beaker in the bathroom at his height. Essential also is a wooden step-up in front of the washstand; don't let the salesman talk you into buying a musical one that starts to tinkle "Of Thee I Sing" when he steps onto it in the morning, or you'll give him the first fright of a day that will have plenty of them as it is. If he is too old for a high chair, get a little booster seat which, strapped to a normal chair, will make him a member of your family at table and not a cliff-hanger.

There are a thousand things you can do in preparation for his arrival; don't let yourself be dissuaded from going to town on this. Your husband, in the meantime, will go alone through a dark and lonesome valley, down the somber road of all expectant fathers. How they survived, none of them ever remembers; but they always emerge, somehow, at the other end in a burst of incoherent elation with the age-old cry, "Have a baby! My wife just had a cigar!"

4

The Arrival

YOUR child will almost certainly arrive by plane, so you will be at the airport to meet him, and again the mother will take the emotional brunt of the occasion.

If what most women experience in those moments goes for you too, you will have the feeling that you are being lived rather than living. For months you have lived toward this moment, untold tension, panic, fear and joy have gone into its making; now here you are, in the lounge at the airport, and the only comfort you have is that you are not alone. Most children arrive in convoys of six or ten; there will be other parents waiting with you, every single one of them looking as nervous and somehow unsuitable as you. Most of them are holding dolls or teddy bears, new and too large; mothers who are expecting infants are carrying baby blankets, bottle-warmers and cute little knitted bonnets with silk ribbons that soon may seem ludicrous if the convoy comes from Vietnam, as the scalps of most children in orphanages over there are infected with one of the fungi endemic in those institutions. The infection itself is not serious, but the Vietnamese treatment consists of painting their heads with a copper-sulfate solution so copiously that they end up by looking like the green roofs of old churches.

Before the arrival there will be delays. Airlines persist in perpetuating the myth that airplanes are so reliable by now that they alight at 10:27 P.M., on the dot, after taking off the previous day at 2:34 sharp from an airfield on the other side of the globe. The plane will be late; a man with a peaked cap will cross the room, carrying a sheaf of papers, muttering angrily that an essential document on some child is missing and you will be convinced it is your own. Among the scores of papers covered with mysterious Chinese characters you are holding, one must be missing, or the wrong name has been inserted, or the one with the red seal, the ribbons and the signature of the Vice Consul in Seoul will turn out to belong to another child. You would burst into tears on your husband's shoulder if it weren't for the presence of those other people and, above all, the social worker, who at this point seems to radiate relaxed self-confidence.

Then, at last, when you are so numbed by emotional exhaustion that the whole thing seems remote and unreal, the arrival of the plane is announced and you run with the others to the window to see it come down from the clouds, belching black smoke, obviously heading for a crash. It vanishes from sight behind distant hangars, but finally there it comes; disembodied little hands are waving behind some of its windows while the man with the yellow signals on the tarmac beckons it into position.

What follows depends on how the convoy of children is made up and who accompanies it. Sometimes the children come marching down the ramp waving little paper flags and singing; at other times they are carried down, yowling or solemnly staring, by stewardesses. One among you will be the first to cry, "There's mine!" and rush through the forbidden barrier. It is guarded by a representative of the airline who has stated that nobody will be allowed to proceed beyond this point, but these imperious bureaucratic arrangements collapse messily the moment mothers set eyes on their children; I have never yet seen an official able to intervene.

You will feel very close to your fellow parents by then; after all those hours it will seem that you have made friends for life with whom, from now on, you will be sharing all your impressions. But the moment you are holding the child you will forget everybody and everything around you and be alone in the world with that pathetic little bundle of life, now trembling against you in heartbreaking terror.

No one knows what the child feels when, after a traumatic voyage through the night in the belly of a giant bird, he is finally put in the arms of a strange woman he will know henceforth as his mother. Some say it is a moment as important as birth; others, that by then he is so stunned and numbed by the bewildering trip and so tired that nothing gets through to him any more. But there can be no doubt as to what this moment means to you: it is like surfacing out of the depths of a lake of dreams into reality. We men will never really know when we crossed the borderline; to a woman reality begins the moment she feels the child's body against hers.

The rest of the voyage will be hazy in your memory; but you will remember the realization that from now on, whatever happens to you and whatever life has in store, you will be going through it together.

We men live through these hours as best we can. We look awkward and feel a little silly; during the long trip home and the first hours of that hectic night we try to be helpful and do not really succeed. When at last all is over and we lie staring in the dark of our bedroom, the realization will dawn on us that the child she has talked about so far as "ours" is not ours at all, but hers. We suspect, with the wry smile of the stoic, that from now on he will be called "your son" only if he has done something wrong. We cannot know yet as we lie there, lonelier than we have ever been before, that the day is near when we will ask ourselves how we could ever have thought we knew the full meaning of being married, before he arrived.

You had better be prepared for it, men: that first night you will get little sleep, so see to it that you get some beforehand. Another tip: before you leave for the airport, put your favorite snack in the icebox, the one that makes you fat and gives you heartburn and that you haven't touched for months with a pallid feeling of virtue. There is nothing like a huge piece of pecan pie à la mode with whipped cream for a man who has to come to terms at dead of night with a bleak, lonely future. Not only will it bolster your ego with a gratifying sense of sin, the heartburn will give you a real cause for self-pity when you lie on your back in the dark again, worrying about fatherhood.

5

The First Night

THE first night, you may be in for a trying initiation.
You bring into your home a child used to sleeping on the
floor in the presence of his family; to put him in a bed by
himself, in a room that, whatever its size, will to him appear enormous, cannot help but cause anxiety and sometimes acute distress.

Some parents have found it necessary to spend the first
night with their new son or daughter on mattresses on
the floor; others took the trembling child into their own
bed; yet others found it was sufficient, if there were
other children in the family, to put all the kids on the
floor, a treat to the old and a comfort to the new. Whatever you do, do not be upset by your child's violent reaction when you insist on putting him in a bed and covering him with bedclothes before turning off the light and
leaving him alone in the dark. He may not like to be covered with blankets and sheets; our elder daughter, for a

long time after she had grown accustomed to a bed, could not stand the sleek, unfamiliar touch of sheets and insisted on sleeping between blankets. The bedroom door may have to be left open, a night light on, not only in his room but in the corridor as well, and the door to your bedroom ajar. This may be necessary for a long time; while during the daytime he may seem to be well adjusted and at ease in his new surroundings, at bedtime you may discover that the battle for adjustment has not been won but merely gone to ground. You must allow him to be the sole judge of his readiness for the dark room, the closed door and the luxury of solitude.

You may discover that pajamas or nighties are unfamiliar items too; if he wants to sleep in his underpants or just a vest, let him; let him go into the night in any way he wants to, for what he is actually doing with his dithering and dallying, his indecision as to whether he wants a pillow or no, is to arm himself for the trial of the long, lonely night, the menacing shadows of uncertainty and fear, the black corners from which the bats of terror may come swooping.

Once he is bedded down, make your leavetaking leisurely and your farewell a kiss blown from your hand, not the little wave of goodbye your own children may be accustomed to. One parent, distraught with worry, took his new Asian son of two weeks' standing to a child psychiatrist because every night, after he had been put to bed happy and contented and nodded enthusiastically at his father's admonition to stay where he was, he would burst into uncontrollable, shrieking sobs the moment the father waved goodbye and vanished into the corridor. The psychiatrist was still probing for the explanation of the nightly ordeal when the mother happened to mention it to an experienced neighbor with Korean children of her own. "Good heavens!" the woman cried, aghast. "No wonder he acts that way! What to us is a wave of goodbye is to him the command 'Come here!' He must have thought he was going crazy!"

During the first night and the following day the child may also be suffering from an upset stomach, resulting in vomiting or diarrhea. In the latter case his stools may look so alarming that you will be tempted to call your doctor out of his bed. Usually, this is the result of the unfamiliar food he has been given during the flight; if we adults occasionally have problems digesting the standard airplane fare, you can imagine what it must do to the intestines of a child who has lived on rice and rice-water for most of his life. If he comes from Vietnam, the nuns in the orphanage may have given him a treat before he departed, like the last dinner of a person about to be hanged, and "treat" in an orphanage usually means fish soup with noodles. The fish part would be considered putrid by our finicky taste, the noodles are indigestible; when expelled from his poor, gas-racked body they will look like the most horrifying worms you ever saw.

Let me reassure you that, once the first traumatic nights are over, your child from Asia, in pleasant contrast with other children, will probably sleep a full twelve hours without stirring, at least for the next three months or so. You put him to bed at seven, read him a story whether he understands it or not, hug him, kiss him good-night and he is likely to sleep soundly until seven the next morning.

This is not a national characteristic or a symptom of

placidity, it is the equivalent of the long periods of restorative sleep needed by a newborn infant. In a most real sense, your child is in the process of being reborn. Every impression he receives during the daytime is a new one which he has to absorb and come to terms with; every experience is unfamiliar, every confrontation with you, his new parents, a test which will determine your future relationship. After such a day filled with challenges, it is not surprising that, like the infant in its cradle, he instantly sinks into the deep, motionless sleep of the emotionally exhausted.

Once his need of restorative baby-sleep is past, you are likely to be confronted with the normal bedtime battle. All parents of young children are battle-scarred veterans in this respect; the last thing you need is my advice. Every parent has his own way of waging that battle and ultimately winning it, only to discover that what looked like a victory was no more than a truce. True peace will not come until the age of discretion.

6

The First Panic

MAYBE you are so experienced, well balanced or just plain lucky that this will not apply to you; the majority of us however are, within the first few days of the arrival of our new child from Asia, likely to go through a blind, witless panic. It will not last long, but it is an experience that none of us will ever forget. The worst of it is—at least, it was in my experience—that it takes you completely unawares and that while it lasts you are convinced it will last forever. I, for one, would have benefited greatly had I known at the time that this ghastly, shattering panic was common in my situation, and that all it took for it to blow over was time.

It rarely strikes both parents at the same moment. There seems to be a natural balance by which one parent can afford to go into a flat spin because the other will instantly rally with a calm and benign—be it faintly self-satisfied—serenity. The only strong emotions that we can safely share are joy and gratitude; as to the rest, we instinctively take turns.

Our two little daughters did not arrive together, but with an interval of several weeks between. The people with whom they were originally placed and who had, owing to circumstances beyond their control, asked that the children be removed, thought at first they would be able to keep the younger one, so it was Eva who arrived first.

I had met her before. When it became apparent that the first couple would not be able to keep her, the director of the adoption agency, with whom I had cooperated on many occasions, went to discuss the situation with the parents. I happened to come into her office just as she was about to leave; she took me along with her. Obviously the discussion could not be held in the presence of the child, so I took Eva out for ice cream; there seemed to be no drugstore around, and we ended up in a dilapidated and rather disreputable-looking diner off the highway. She spoke very little English at the time, but we got along very well. I drew manikins and doggies on the back of an envelope, even wrote underneath, "mommy" and "dog." Her ice cream was so hard that every time she tried to push the spoon into the clay-like substance the seat of the bar stool on which she sat turned around. I was impressed by her poise, her dignity and her awareness. If ever a child was trapped in a desperate situation, it was she at that moment; there are few things worse to a child from Asia than to be rejected by her new parents on whom she has concentrated all her hopes and dreams for months and on whom she has counted for protection in the frightening, alien unknown; even if the need to place her with another family arises from an act of God like illness or death, the child will experience it as a rejection. This, on top of everything else she had gone through, must have been a harrowing experience for the little girl; yet there she sat, calm and composed, perched on her stool, manfully trying to cope with her ice cream; from time to time she even tried by a smile or a nod to put the insecure old man by her side at his ease, as he sat there blubbering frantic baby-talk, drawing piggies. What struck me most was her readiness, at the age of five, to identify with someone else and to ease his embarrassment by merely being aware of it.

That evening after dinner I wrote down my impressions of her, stressing her awareness, which had seemed so remarkable and so far ahead of her age, hoping that by doing so I might give her potential future parents an idea of her extraordinary personality.

A few days later, in the late afternoon, the telephone rang. It was the director of the agency. A new crisis in the home had made it necessary to remove the little girl at once. There was no couple as yet prepared to take the child in on a permanent basis, so she asked if we would put her up for a few weeks, maybe a month, while a new placement was being arranged. We answered that of course we would. Our house, which we had rented specifically as a staging area for Vietnamese orphans, had twenty rooms in all; no orphans had arrived thus far, so there was plenty of space. Marjorie was not well at the time and had to stay in bed, but we felt that to have a little girl staying with us on a temporary basis would be no hardship.

She arrived that same night, delivered by three

women: the director of the agency, a fellow social worker and a friend. They had heard about Marjorie's illness and kindly volunteered to cook a meal while I occupied myself with the little girl. I will never forget the way she came in: small and brave, but obviously badly shaken. She carried a little plastic pocketbook, which later turned out to contain thirteen cents; the rest of her worldly belongings were packed in a cardboard box, carried in by the director.

The moment I saw her and she saw me, I realized with a sinking feeling in my stomach that we were fooling ourselves if we thought of this as temporary. The feeling was not pity, although I was deeply moved by the realization that Marjorie and I were now all she had in the world to turn to; it was a sense of destiny, the sudden realization which occasionally comes to us that a seemingly unimportant event will change the course of our lives.

Marjorie had come down to welcome her, and lay on the couch in the living room in her robe. The little girl was formally introduced to her; again I was struck by the child's poise and awareness. But Marjorie told me later that when they shook hands the child's had trembled, desperately; during the evening I suspected several times that her gaiety and restlessness masked nervousness and fear. When I asked her, a year later, how she had felt that night when she first came into our home, she answered, casually, "Scared." By her very nonchalance it was obvious that, even after all this time, she still did not want to talk about it.

She was not the only one who was scared. While Marjorie seemed to be quite unaffected, I felt myself shaking

like a leaf. Maybe it was because she called me "Daddy";
I did not know at the time that this is what Korean children call any man for a while after their arrival, the way
they will call any woman "Mummy."

The three kind women, rather overpowering at that
moment in their jolly, robust decisiveness, set about making supper. I was sent to get a carton of eggs and an extra
half gallon of milk. Because of the hour, the only place
where I could get these things was the delicatessen, a mile
or so down the road. I went to the garage and pushed up
the door; that was the moment the panic hit me.

Suddenly, as I stood there in the darkness fumbling for
my car keys, my knees gave way. I leaned against the wall,
overwhelmed by a sudden wave of despair that made me
cover my face with my hands. I saw my pleasant, well-
organized life collapse in confusion. This meant the end
of the intimate relationship I had had with Marjorie all
those years. Everything I cherished and cared for—my
peace, my middle-aged comfort, my serenity—was shat-
tered by this stranger calling me "Daddy." On the one
hand I knew that I could never send her away again, to
face yet another set of parents with that heartbreaking
poise and frightening awareness; on the other hand I
knew that I simply could not bear this—this mess, this
disorganization, this invasion of my privacy, this destruc-
tion of the close and exclusive relationship with my wife.
I took the car out and drove to the delicatessen; I roamed
along the counters feeling old and hysterical, utterly unsuitable to be anybody's father, let alone an Asian child's.
But I meekly got the eggs, a dozen, grade A large, and
the half gallon of fortified milk. I wound my way back
to the house along a detour that I had never taken be-

fore, a pathetic last effort to stay the execution.

The rest of that night is hazy in my memory. I know there came a moment when I felt the urge to go out into the garden and scream before I could sit down at the table with some semblance of composure, but I didn't. I chatted, chuckled and chortled my idiotic way through that interminable evening until, finally, the three women left, waved off by the little girl on my arm in the doorway. Then I closed the door and there we were, the three of us, alone.

Marjorie and I put her to bed together. I cannot remember what we talked about after we had left her small and alien little form in the big bed and gone to our own room. My panic had subsided somewhat, but it had been replaced by a dull, sullen hopelessness from which I sought refuge by swallowing a couple of sleeping pills, and I soon keeled over into oblivion.

When I woke early the next morning, the sense of being trapped by my own folly was undiminished. I could not discern a single ray of hope or promise in the day that stretched drearily ahead of me, or in the endless, dreary days to come. I had, for years, been the first to get up. I would go down to the kitchen, make a cup of tea and take it up to Marjorie with the morning paper. I did so without any sense of drudgery or virtue; I liked it that way. It gave me a chance to prepare for the day at my ease and on my own terms; it gave her a chance to start it in comfort and relaxation. Now, suddenly, there was a strange child in the house; although I did not yet know how to go about waking her or how she would fit into the morning, one thing was certain: the pleasant routine of ages, now so nostalgically revealed as infinitely dear to me and indispensable for my peace of mind and joy of living, was a thing of the past. Heaven knew what the rest of my mornings would be like; certainly neither serene, leisurely nor intimate. Well, I had better get on with it. I got out of bed, opened the door to the landing quietly, so as not to wake up the sleeping child in the room opposite, and suddenly there she was: sitting at the top of the stairs in her pajamas, an image of loneliness. Her face looked so forlorn, she sat there so crushed and defeated, that before I could catch myself I went toward her, knelt by her side and asked, "What's the matter? What happened?" She looked at me with an unforgettable expression of despair, but said nothing. I touched her cheek and felt it was stone-cold; she must have been sitting there for hours.

I lifted up her stolid little body and held it against me and carried her into our bedroom; she was so cold that I woke up Marjorie. "Sorry, dear," I said, "I'll bring your tea in a moment, but here . . . Maybe you can warm her first."

Marjorie, with the instant presence of mind sailors and nurses share, opened her bed. I put the child down beside her and covered them both with the blanket. When I turned around in the doorway and saw the small dark patch of hair on Marjorie's shoulder, I knew that something had been settled. I went downstairs, made the tea, added a beaker of milk and a cookie; then, followed by the two dogs who were part of the ceremony and had been for years, I carried the tray upstairs, put it down on the bedside table, opened the curtains and said, "Good morning, girls." The plural came naturally; it has been so ever since.

7

The First Meal

A DIETICIAN in the Netherlands, who doubted the wisdom of adopting Asian children, did so because, on top of all other bewildering changes, these children would have to get used to an entirely different cuisine. When I asked her what specifically she thought would be so different, she answered, "Isn't their taste terribly carnivorous? For instance, in this country we never eat dog."

This seemed a surprising statement for a representative of a nation that licks its lips at the mere mention of fried cow's udder, roast suckling pig, poached lamb's brains or boiled Australian groper, head and shoulders, of which the thick, glutinous lips are considered to be a special delicacy. Other than cornering the screaming cook himself and sinking her fangs into his succulent Flemish posterior, I wondered what carnivorous heights the good lady imagined there were left to scale.

One thing is certain: you need not give away your dog

before your child arrives, for fear that he will assume you are fattening Fido for the pot. The menu in the orphanages of Vietnam is rice, if they are lucky, otherwise rice-water and any bit of fish, meat or vegetable that can be scrounged. In Korea they are better off by now; but even to a Korean child the danger is that our diet will turn out to be too rich and heavy for him. Several parents reported that their new children, especially the very young ones, were stricken with an alarming and persistent diarrhea within hours of their arrival; doctors were stumped by the mysterious ailment until they realized that the children could not digest the rich American milk. The milk was stopped and the diarrhea vanished; so this may be a point to remember.

Your child's first meal under your roof is likely to be breakfast. Of course, you are eager to put him at ease. Your overriding desire is to comfort him, to compensate for past deprivations, still so clearly visible in his solemn face, his old eyes, his pathetically thin arms, his distended belly. In your eagerness, you may cause him distress by the very demonstration of your generosity and good intentions.

We made this mistake ourselves. That first morning we put in front of our five-year-old little daughter the full cornucopia of the American breakfast table. Four kinds of cereal, boiled eggs, toast, fruit, muffins—she sat facing the display with expressionless eyes, hands in her lap, frozen in an inexplicable paralysis. We did not know at the time that this face was not her own but a mask and that her self-contained composure was not impassiveness but terror; in our innocence, we failed to realize that by demonstrating our delight at her presence in this way we had thrown her into anguish and confusion. To face her with this plethora of affluence was not giving her a choice but burdening her with responsibility; what we should have done was to give her what we ourselves were eating: cereal and an apple. Once she had settled down in the routine of our family and felt secure enough for experiments in independence, we could have widened the choice to two cereals, an apple and a banana.

As long as you avoid this error, you will find your first meal with your new son or daughter to be an unexpectedly moving experience. It is not for nothing that most tribes to which we refer as "primitive" attach a symbolic value to the breaking of bread with a stranger; a remnant of this tradition is left in the Holy Communion.

Its mystical meaning will be discerned by you, as in a glass darkly, when you and your child face each other across your table for his first meal in his new fatherland.

8

Language

You may have worried about this before his arrival, especially if he is at the articulate age. How are you going to communicate with him? How long will it take before you will be able to exchange anything except signs and smiles? Will he have an accent for the rest of his life?

In the order of appearance, the answer to these questions are as follows. You must, before the child arrives, get hold of a simple traveler's dictionary or, failing that, a list of the most common words from your adoption agency: "food," "bed," "toilet," "no." After the first twenty-four hours you will find that you communicate surprisingly well in sign language. There can be no mistaking the gestures of hospitality, concern and friendliness; as he will be observing you like a lynx, you must realize that your slightest frown will be as disapproving as your most casual smile will be encouraging. Especially if there are other children in your family or in the neighborhood, his vocabulary will grow apace—so fast, as a matter of fact, that you are likely to forget his English does not as yet cover abstract aspects of daily living like "late," "far" or "tomorrow." For many months one of our daughters could express distance in time in the future only by stretching the second syllable of "tomorrow." The day after tomorrow would be called "tomo-orrow," next week "tomo-----orrow," while "in the distant future," which covered anything from a week onward, would be expressed by stretching the second "o" for as long as her breath would hold.

As to the accent, you need not worry. Most children arrive young enough to absorb our language until it sounds as if it were their native tongue. Only in the case of older and crustier creatures like myself will the astute listener be able to situate the land of our birth for the rest of our days.

One thing you must be prepared for: as a price for the acquisition of English, your child will completely forget his own mother tongue. Korean children, after only a few months in the United States, will not remember a single word of Korean; it seems as if one language wipes out the other on the magnetic tape of their memory. When after a while he shrugs his shoulders at your question, "What is the word for that in Korean?" he is not being uncooperative, he simply no longer knows.

9

The First Hurdle-1

(CHILDREN FROM 2 TO 4)

IT may be as early as the very first day, but more likely it will come a few days after his arrival. Despite the first impression he gave you, his new mother, and in alarming contradiction to the simple trust and acceptance with which he nestled in your arms during the drive home from the airport, your child may suddenly shrink from all physical contact, turn balky and sullen, and glower at you when you ingratiate yourself. In a most disconcerting way he seems to divine your secret thought, even before it has actually risen to the surface of your consciousness: "No use denying it, there must be a basic incompatibility between me and this strange little boy. For six months I dreamed of him as my very own son, and there he stands—a total stranger, almost an enemy."

What has happened? Is it your fault? Is it his? The

explanation for this deeply upsetting but fairly common situation lies in those six months of dreaming, not only on your part but also on his. During that time each of you has, so gradually that it went unnoticed, come to idealize the other. Your meeting after all those months was the apotheosis of the most untrammeled daydream either of you had ever had. Now the sober confrontation of your realities is taking place; today, in contrast with the hundreds of days that went before, is not one more step closer to the goal of your union, but the first step on the empty road of the future, stretching drearily into infinity. How do you cope with this?

If your child is young enough, simply pick him up and carry him on your hip for the rest of the day. He may shrink from physical contact when it is clearly intended as a caress; to this he will respond with eagerness, as it does not demand the effort of a response on his part but is merely the ancestral way in which any Asian mother carries her child.

For yourself, the thing to do is to flee into small, comforting everyday activities which, by the very fact that they are part of an established routine, will exude a sense of security. You may be a mess as a mother, but you know that you are a capable housekeeper; now is the time to rally around you all the self-confidence you can muster on the most basic plane of daily living. Neither you nor the child will derive any sense of security from the fact that you have a master's degree in business administration or took down a hundred and fifty words a minute in your prime; neither your gift for languages nor your social graces will be any good to you in this first test of your proficiency as a mother. The gradual conviction of the reality of your motherhood will come, to you as well as to him, from the ease with which you perform basic little tasks like washing up, putting away the dishes, making the beds, greeting the milkman, feeding the dog. Meanwhile, the unyielding little body on your hip may seem to regard your efforts at efficiency with hostile scorn; but as you carry him, going about the chores and pleasures of your everyday life, you and he will be touching in some symbolic manner the confines of your world, small as it may be. It is from this review of the boundaries of your territory that he will receive his first, tenuous reassurance. His deepest wish, his most compelling urge is to surrender to you, to accept the security of your affection, the protection of your strength. If you can see this first, harrowing day as a survey of your world for his benefit, you will have taken the first step on a road that will, ultimately, lead to a very real relationship between the two of you. Out of these inconspicuous beginnings may grow something deeper, more far-reaching, than if you and he were related by blood.

So basic are his needs, so elemental is the nature of your relationship, that your staunchest allies are the small, inconspicuous rituals of daily life which, for some years now, you have often considered sheer drudgery. Maybe this is why many children from the Orient seem to remember in later years that they first met their new mother in the kitchen.

10

The First Hurdle-2

(CHILDREN FROM 5 TO 8)

In the case of the older child too it may come at any moment, even the first day. Any seemingly innocent confrontation between him and you as his mother may trigger it. He points at a piece of candy, you shake your head; he opens the door to go out into the garden, you hold him back to put on his coat; however puny the pretext, the implosion that follows will be monumental and unnerving. It is an implosion, not an explosion: he will suddenly freeze into total motionlessness, and there is nothing more obstinate or more able to make it stick than our Asian children in stance number one: Lot's Wife.

The tricky part of the situation is your reaction. You are still insecure and nervous after the emotional experience of the recent past; you don't love him yet for what he is; now there he stands by the kitchen table: hostile, remote, immovably implanted in his imperious determination not to budge ever, not ever. Don't force him to obey or pick him up, don't pander to him either. Just say, in English, without any effort at ingratiating pidgin, "Sorry, John, that's the way it's going to be, boy. I think you're a fine fellow and we are happy to have you with us, but there's one boss around here, and that is I." After that, go calmly about your business, turning your back on him in the hope that he will not notice the shaking of your hands as you start to do something pointless, like putting a breakfast plate in a Baggie, or slicing an onion. What have you done to bring this about? All you want, desperately want, is to love him, to make up to him for all that has gone before, and there he stands, the little monster, rejecting you, taunting you. He has been here less than twenty-four hours and already the battle is on as to who is going to run whom. You have been warned by other parents that boys from Korea consider women to be inferior to them, some may start out with the notion that you are supposed to wait on them. Well, he has a surprise coming! Or has he . . . ?

If you can bring yourself to do it, go away. Leave the kitchen, let him stand there and see where it gets him. It will get him exactly where he wants to be: brought up short by a fence. Any horse-trainer will tell you that when an animal is put out to pasture in an unfamiliar meadow, it will not calm down and feel secure until it has tested the fence along the full periphery; only after it has convinced itself that it cannot get out will it deign to graze. Your child is compelled by the same instinctive urge when, after his own fashion, he challenges you to tell him where the fence is, where you say "No." You are the fixed point in his universe; it is from this point that he will, as Pythagoras said twenty-five centuries ago, ultimately be able to move the earth.

It's simple: all you have to be is the fixed point in his universe. I know what you would rather be, right now: a helpless, sensitive, tender female, a gentle, loving mother. It's a pity that your husband is at the office all day; it's a pity that you have to impersonate Tugboat Annie before you can be allowed to become a mother. But then, if Eve hadn't taken over where Adam left off, man would still be dangling in the trees of Paradise and Pythagoras would still be a dream in the mind of God.

So, go away and let him stew in his own juice. You must leave him after saying "No," or he will lose face. We frequently put our children in a situation from which they simply cannot extricate themselves. If one of my daughters pouts or sulks and I tell her to smile and be sociable or have her meal by herself in the kitchen, then she simply cannot make the transition from the sullen child to the sociable one unless I help her do so. This means in most instances simply sending her out of the room to get her apron or a book—any little errand will do; she will come back radiant and as sociable as a hostess. Had I nailed her to the spot, she would have had no choice but to go on sulking more glumly or, worse, obey with the smile of the hyena.

You can't send the boy out of the kitchen, so you'll have to leave the kitchen yourself; when you come back, chances are that he will leap at you from a hiding place crying "Boo!"; and you had better react with gay surprise, even if he scares you to the point where you feel like wringing his neck.

11

Is Psychiatric Help Needed?

IN rare cases, especially if the child is older, things may
get so rough for a while that you as his mother will seriously ask yourself whether he doesn't need psychiatric
help.

There are indeed instances known where children
from Asia have benefited from sessions with a child psychiatrist, and even if the child's benefit was open to question, there can be no doubt that the parents felt a whole
lot better. But before you go, it may be helpful if I mention a few common symptoms, just to put your mind at
ease.

To start with: the frozen face of the inscrutable East.
Virtually all Asian children will, when confronted with a
situation that calls for added adrenalin, hide behind this
expressionless mask and create the impression of an almost schizoid retreat from reality. In a Western child this
sudden removal of the self from the scene, while the smil-

ing body stays behind, could give cause for concern; in Asian children it just happens to be the way they react to situations of stress. Do not be alarmed or put out by apparent hostility either. It's highly unlikely that it is indeed hostility; more likely it is the child's psychological defense mechanism, alerted by the first twinges of a growing weakness inside him. The past has forced him to defend himself against emotional invasions from the outside. The greatest danger to the lone wolf, which is the characteristic personality of the winner in the battle for survival, is for him to become emotionally dependent on someone else. Physical dependence is not a threat—the lone wolf cub assumes that he can always look after himself when it comes to scrounging food and shelter; emotional dependence is something else again. To counter his wariness and instinctive reluctance you should, once again, activate your bovine qualities. If you happen to be a mercurial, extrovert personality, you may have some difficulty impersonating a placid cow. If you can't do so without strangling all spontaneity, don't worry about it. Sincerity is important, to be physically present is important. To be psychologically adept would help, but it is not essential.

The essentially important thing is honesty. You cannot be expected to love him at this point—he is still a stranger whose presence has turned out to be more upsetting and whose personality more complicated than you had anticipated. He knows that unless he makes a success of your relationship his outlook for the future is full of menace. But he cannot help himself; his past has conditioned him to respond to your readiness to like him, to make him your son, with a feeling of panic at his own yearning to be dependent, to be a child. To give in to your siren call would mean to hand over his only weapon, aggressiveness, and the removal of his armor, indifference. Who knows how many times in the past he has been coaxed out of the fortress of his self-containment, only to be rejected? Who knows how often, overwhelmed by his yearning to be a child, he has allowed himself to reach out with affection to some adult, some passing stranger, who involuntarily seduced him with a smile or a gesture of kindness and then recoiled from the desperate intensity of the emotional response it provoked? Each time the child must have decided, be it inarticulately, that this would not happen to him again; and here you are, with your kindness, your readiness to give him all the things he craves: shelter, affection, warmth, security; no wonder his reaction is to shrink and draw away. The degree to which he has bricked himself in depends on his past and his individual character, but to some degree all of these children have drawn a circle. around themselves in the sand and can cross it only with a sense of recklessness.

The danger about bringing in professional help is that it introduces another person into what is, essentially, a matter between you and him. The fact that his inner battle has been triggered by you and is focused on you is your greatest strength. It is worth considering whether, rather than bringing in another person, you should not do what experienced hunters and shepherds do when they get a new dog: they vanish into the hills or woods and stay there alone with the young animal until a shadow line is crossed which separates the "you and I" from the "we." You will undoubtedly have an easier time getting to know each other if you can limit outside interference to a minimum. For this you need not go so far as to isolate yourselves on a boat on the lake or a cabin in the mountains. Just explain to your friends and relatives that, much as you would love them to meet your new son, it will be best if he is given a week or so to settle down before being exposed to the strains and distractions of new faces.

Give yourself and your husband a chance to isolate yourselves with your new child by doing something together with him, each of you in turn, like raking the garden, watering the lawn, washing the car or taking the rowboat out to go fishing. Not a word needs to be spoken, no gesture of affection made; just give the child and yourselves a chance to get used to each other's physical presence, which is a bridge you'll have to cross before there can be an encounter.

12

Clinging

ONCE you, his mother, have cleared this hurdle and his shrinking from physical contact is over (the older the child, the longer this will take), you will suddenly find yourself confronted with a hunger on his part for physical closeness, so ravenous and insatiable that chances are you may end by being sincerely worried whether there isn't something psychologically wrong with him. Even to the most extrovert and sensual among us there comes a point beyond which the need for being hugged, caressed, kissed and snuggled turns from an uninhibited desire for affection into an obsession that soon makes us do the opposite of what we are so breathlessly urged to do: we draw away in alarm and confusion.

I have not heard of a single exception to this rule: all children from Korea or Vietnam are literally starved for affection; once they surrender themselves to you, there is no moderation or restraint until their desperate craving is satisfied and they have made up in the space of a few months for the emotional deprivation of a lifetime.

Those few months are likely to be trying. In the beginning you may enjoy his total and unrelenting claim on your full and constant attention. But the desperate tightness with which especially the very young child will clasp your leg, clutch your arm, cling to your neck until you have to carry him with you from morning to night may well alarm you. The thing is to try and relax. Let yourself be kissed, hugged, nuzzled, nibbled and beset by frenzied embraces like any simian mother, whom you can observe in any zoo. Your colleague among the gorillas, orangutans or baboons goes about her monkey business totally oblivious of the huge-eyed, frantic young clinging to her breast, waist or even tail with all the symptoms of utter terror. She climbs trees with him, stuffs herself with peanuts while he dangles from her neck, gossips while he peers over her shoulder, and all she ever does in recognition of his presence is to inspect his thin and fluffy fur for salt crystals, which she disposes of by consumption.

I do not suggest that you should emulate the monkey mother's actions, but you should try and attain her attitude. You will have to resign yourself to the circumstance that, for the next few months, you will be carrying a small shivering body attached like a leech to some part of your person during most of your waking hours and, once he has overcome his initial exhaustion, your sleeping hours as well. There is no harm in talking about this to your doctor, there is no harm in talking about it to anybody. But I assure you that his behavior is normal; it would be abnormal if he were not to show this frantic hunger for affection.

There will be moments when his clinging seems to intensify, as if he were suddenly overcome by the fear of losing you. At those times, take a leaf from the book of experienced nannies, who have discovered that there is one sure way to make a small child relax and that is to talk to him. It's not necessary that he understand a single word of what you say; he is not interested in what you say, he is interested in the way you say it. I will never forget an old and formidable supervisor of nurses who, when my wife first started work some years ago in a Southern charity hospital, would enter the newborn nursery looking like an ogre. Suddenly, as she approached the first row of bassinettes, she would emit a high-pitched, incomprehensible stream of utter twaddle, coo and babble words no dictionary lists, all at the same level of voice and in the same volume. She made the rounds of the babies in the ward, babbling all the time; wherever she went, all crying would cease, shrieks, sobs and heaving desperation would turn into toothless grins, the drunken waving of newborn fists, the frantic pedaling of pudgy bow legs that gave her the full benefit of the cyclist's first fruity diaper. She had no patience with, confidence in or tenderness for anyone over the age of three months, but when it came to babies, still cross-eyed and punch drunk after the great transition, she was motherhood incarnate and could do for sixty apoplectic screechers what many women find themselves incapable of doing for one.

I once had a cup of coffee with her, at dead of night. It was at the height of an epidemic of salmonella which affected especially the premature babies, utterly helpless in their incubators. I don't know whether exhaustion had mollified her or the mere fact of my being around at that hour, but she relented sufficiently to tell me, apropos of nothing, that any frightened child will respond to the soothing voice of any motherly woman, on condition she keeps it up until he has calmed down. For whatever it's worth, I pass on this information; if in your case it turns out to be nonsense, it will be one more proof that even the most level-headed saint may not have a clue as to the true secret of her powers.

13

Routine

BEFORE he can relax and begin to explore his new world, your Asian child will need the security of a firmly established daily routine. All children need it, as every mother knows: if you read them a story one night, you have to read them a story every night; if you interrupt this comforting recurrence of the expected, the night is likely to be a memorable one. Asian children, displaced as they are, need this soothing timetable desperately, and they will be determined to establish it as soon as possible, if need be off their own bat.

So be sure, during the first days and weeks, to realize that everything you do, good or bad, popular or unpopular, will instantly be added to the timetable. The way you awaken him in the morning, the sequence in which you put on his clothes, the visit to the toilet, the washing of hands, the brushing of teeth—he will want to turn everything into a tradition and you should help him do so. If you give him a table mat with a certain picture on it for breakfast, don't give him another one the next day, for you'll distress him. He may hate cereal, but once he has eaten one kind at breakfast he will go on eating it even though it sticks in his gullet, because the comfort of the routine exceeds his distaste for the crunchy stuff. He will go on wearing the same pair of sneakers until you have to remove them forcibly for fear his feet will become stunted; everything from the hour the milkman knocks to the place where Daddy puts his reading glasses in the living room—all is transformed into a perpetuum mobile by the child, desperate for consistency. So desperate that, seen from the snug security of our family pew in the universe, he may seem almost demented in his demands that every daily occurrence down to the smallest minutia shall be repeated today exactly as it happened yesterday and that ad infinitum, until you could scream.

Bear with it, enjoy it if you can, for what you are witnessing is the secret of man's survival itself; so, one day in the unimaginable past, a lonely homunculus cast out by his tribe must have uncurled his frail little body from the fetal position in which he had crouched in his terror, to stand up and face the world, determined to live.

In memory of that little man, father of us all, please put the folded paper napkin on the wrong side of his plate, if this is what you did the first day, and make sure that the small glass of milk is on the right side and the orange juice on the left. Do it consciously, with deliberation, for it will be to him your first gesture of affection. To hug him and kiss him and tuck him in and tell him how happy you are he is here hasn't meant a thing to the trembling, overwrought child who suddenly found himself among the Martians; the paper napkin is a symbol, the first word you speak in his language. For though no one may be able to give a full definition of "love," this much we know: it begins with an act of identification.

14

Bed-wetting

In most of Asia, but especially in Korea, children are house-trained with brutality. Little toddlers barely one year old have it drummed into them, by a corporal punishment that pulls no punches, that to wet their beds is unacceptable. And no wonder. Most families sleep together on the floor; one member, however small, losing control of his reflexes can be a messy business, to say the least. The result is that bed-wetting to most Asian children is a mortal sin.

In our more affluent and therefore more lenient society we have discovered after trial and error that, especially in the child who is no longer a toddler, bed-wetting is an expression of some secret fear or anxiety. So it stands to reason that our children from Asia, at least during the first weeks after their arrival, may have problems in that respect. As in their case it is a subject fraught with terror and violence, I'm inclined to believe that, whatever our own feelings may be, we should show an angelic patience and serenity toward them. You have to prepare yourself for serenity beforehand by getting in a good supply of cheap sheets and a plastic mattress cover; a well-functioning washing machine is an essential condition for sainthood in this instance.

But you must start by realizing the need, often overlooked by adoptive parents, for small children to be lifted and put on the toilet around eleven P.M., as twelve hours is too long for containment. When our children first arrived, I had just reached the age where it becomes necessary for a man to get up during the night, and as our two aging dogs had begun to produce distressing evidence of the same problem, I combined operations. After nature woke me up at dead of night, I would go downstairs to let the dogs out, go upstairs to put the two children on the pot, go back downstairs again to let the dogs in and back to bed with a sense of accomplishment. My early training as a sailor made it second nature to me to start operating, at least physically, the moment my feet hit the floor; I developed the knack of going on sleeping, sometimes for a considerable time, after my body had become operational and started to go through a series of conditioned reflexes all by itself. This led on one occasion to the child I was putting on the pot putting up a vicious struggle; I woke up to realize that it was a dog. The story of Daddy putting Fifi on the pot at dead of night is one of the enduring sagas of our family, the children never tire of it.

Even now, it may occasionally happen that one of our daughters suffers a relapse. We have an arrangement whereby, in that case, she instantly comes to me without

waking up her mother. I get up and help her change the
bed on the consideration that it is better to grumble
through an unwelcome intermission than to have on our
hands a child with a cold which will spread through the
entire family. Occasionally, maybe, the real reason for
the relapse is the subconscious need on her part to see it
reconfirmed that a mortal sin of yore has turned into a
secret midnight giggle.

15

Manners

TABLE manners will present no problem; for some reason this is the first outward aspect of our civilization your child will be at pains to emulate. But you had better read up on your Emily Post before his arrival so that your own manners, once they come under the scrutiny of his beady black eyes, will be the way you want his to be. He will observe how you handle knife and fork at the very first meal. In all probability he will sit there with a deceptive air of remoteness, but don't be taken in by this; tomorrow or the next day you will see, to your astonishment tinged with alarm, that the child from the Stone Age has memorized your manners to the smallest detail and copies them with an elegance you can never hope to attain. The same goes for all forms of behavior; he will observe you first, to avoid doing anything that may not please you, then he will mirror you. And you should definitely allow him to do so for a while, until he understands that he need no longer make the grade.

As far as manners in general are concerned, you will have little cause for concern. There is even a chance that when your child arrives you may be confronted with too much of a good thing; instances are known where a child started out by treating his new parents with unnerving courtesy. It may happen to you; in that case, after an initial reaction of pleasant surprise, you will gradually be overcome by the eerie impression that instead of a helpless child, desperately needing the warmth and the protection of your love, you have a miniature Doctor Fu Manchu on your hands. The only things lacking, so it will seem to you, are a silk robe with sleeves wide enough to hide his hands in, felt-soled shoes and the black cardinal's hat which, in the early days of the motion-picture industry, had the same symbolic meaning the black cowboy hat has in today's westerns. Everything else is there: the bow from the waist, the fixed smile, the immovable face and the black, impenetrable eyes that, if they express anything at all, do not radiate filial affection.

All this, odd as it seems, makes sense. Thrown, all on his own, through the looking glass into a world where everything must seem topsy-turvy to him and all his familiar values have become meaningless, he is rallying around him, like an emotional carapace, every vestige of formality and mannerism he can remember to protect his identity from being overwhelmed. For you to try and prise open the fragile shell of his ridiculous courtesy would defeat your purpose; let him find his own feet and determine for himself his moment of decision. Sooner or later the elemental yearning for the security of parental affection common to all children is bound to overcome his instinctive, mortal fear of losing his bearings, if not his identity.

Yet, this is what he will have to do in the end: give up one identity in exchange for another. The barefoot boy who ran with the pack through the alleys of an old walled city or the streets of an army compound will have to turn into a boy in sneakers, T-shirt and jeans, waiting with his schoolbooks under his arm for the yellow bus with the flashing red lights that will take him to Siloville's First Elementary. The two boys are not the same. The urchin who, arms outstretched, begged for cigarettes or gum from warriors in harness perched on top of a tank rumbling past has little to do with your son, standing there tense and eager with his baseball bat. In a very short time he will begin to forget that other boy so completely that, in a most real sense, you will have to be the safekeeper of his childhood memories; the day will come when you will remember the small and casual details that he told you about his Asian boyhood better than he will himself.

But during the first days after his arrival, there he is: little Mr. Chinatown, smiling and bowing like a television commercial for frozen chow mein. He'll drive you to despair and tears unless you understand what is going on. The best way for you to get a glimpse of the real little boy hidden inside the mechanical doll is to get up at dead of night, tiptoe into his room and look at him as he lies there: eyes closed, mouth open, looking barely two years old. He is younger still; the child you are gazing at is an infant, exhausted by the effort to find an answer to the first question of the newborn in our strange and bewildering world: where am I?

This question no one can answer for him. All you can do to help him in his quest is to be there when he needs you, without any preconceived ideas as to who you would like the stranger to be who so suddenly and bewilderingly has appeared in your home.

16

Cleanliness

You should be glad that the new member of your family has at least one stellar virtue that will become apparent the moment he sets foot in your house: a passion for cleanliness. Because it is a passion, its effects, at least while you are still feeling your way, may be the opposite of what was intended.

Of one thing you can be sure: during the first weeks your new child's foremost desire will be to please you. As he does not yet know your idiosyncrasies, he will try to please you the way he would please his own mother, the nun in charge of his ward if he comes from an orphanage, or the housemother in the reception center. All of these reacted with approval and—who knows?— maybe even a sign of affection when he made a real effort to be clean and neat.

Some years ago, a couple of parents were literally driven to despair by their new Korean son's unbearable neatness. From the first morning on, he would get up at six, clean his room, strip his bed, fold sheets, blankets and eiderdown and put them in a neat stack with the pillow on top; then he would open the window, do a series of exercises of military precision, close the window, go to the bathroom, take a shower and appear at the breakfast table as clean as a whistle, nails pared, hair plastered in the unprepossessing style known as the "Hitler cut," he would stand to attention, speak a guttural greeting, bow from the waist, march to his chair, sit down and wait, motionlessly, staring straight ahead of him, both hands on the table, for his breakfast. Whatever they tried—and they tried for days—the parents were unable to turn this robot of correctness and precision into a human being. Some compulsion, some disturbing streak of insanity seemed to compel him to go through the same movements in exactly the same sequence every God-given morning, until they could have screamed. In the end they called up their social worker and told her, shamefacedly but driven to the point of distraction, that they could not possibly keep this boy. They weren't sure what he needed, maybe another set of parents, maybe psychiatric help, but in their house and under the influence of their obviously uncongenial personalities he behaved like a child with a spell thrown over him, especially during that unbearable ritual in the morning.

The social worker came to see them. They talked it over; she managed to convince them that all the child was trying to do was please them; this was his only means of expressing what he felt. She advised them to take him on a short vacation, preferably camping in a tent; he should be put in a situation where he simply could not obey the pianola roll of the early-morning drill that had been punched into him in some orphanage. The parents, for whom camping was out of the question, compromised by taking their marionette to a motel at the seaside, where in a room with two double beds the apprehensive little boy was put to sleep with his Dad. At the early-morning hour when the secret clockwork in his brain set him off on his compulsive daily dozen, the father calmly but kindly held him back, took him to his mother's bed, turned on the television and there they lay, the three of them, watching Captain Kangaroo, listening to commercial jingles. Gradually, magically, the parents began to feel a blessed relaxation after all those horrible days of growing insecurity and incomprehension. The little boy, after lying there rigid for a long time, finally began to watch the screen; he laughed at a cartoon showing a dialogue between a man and his stomach, and suddenly, unexpectedly, he fell asleep again.

What exactly happened during that sleep, nobody ever knew; but when he woke up a little while later to find himself alone in the big bed and his parents leisurely dressing, he smiled for the first time, a ravishing smile of recognition. When after a few days they took him home, he never again reverted to his old automatic self; he became what every boy of his age will be, to the dismay and exasperation of his parents: an incurable slob.

Without expecting this extreme situation, you must be prepared for an exemplary child whose passion for cleanliness, neatness and order may delight you or make you feel uncomfortable, depending on your own preference. If he makes you uncomfortable, your future is brighter; from the moment he begins to settle down, at the first hesitant sense of security, his exemplary behavior will deteriorate until he ends up—happily or unhappily, whatever your case may be—as a clothes-dropping, antiwashing non-toiletflusher.

Occasionally I hear my wife sigh, "Where for Pete's sake have those beautiful manners gone, that wonderful sense of neatness? We must be a family of tramps to make such well-behaved children start acting like this!"

At which I grunt sympathetically and bury my nose in the paper, feet on the coffee table, hiding the diminutive left shoe that I discovered in my chair as I sat down.

17

Hair

THIS applies only if the child is a girl, in which case it may be important. We stumbled onto it only by chance.

The first adoptive mother of our little girls, undoubtedly with the best intentions, took them to a beauty parlor soon after their arrival and had their waist-length hair cut off and shaped in a more practical fashion.

They never forgave her; until this day the poor woman is referred to by our daughters as "the boy's mother who cut off our hair." Long hair is now almost an obsession with them; they insist on growing it again, much to the chagrin of my wife, who, like the woman in question, feels that here, where they bathe daily in the sea and play in the tangled jungle of our island, they would be better off with their hair as short as possible.

But, obviously, long hair has a great symbolic value to little girls from Asia. It must have been a thing of beauty in the eyes of their natural mother and a lot of care must have been spent on it that, had there been money, would have been spent on clothes. It is something one can indeed only stumble upon by chance; so here is the information, for those among you who may be in a position to profit from an innocent woman's mistake.

18

Shoes

SINCE the war there has been only one standard type of footwear in Asia: the Japanese thongs made of rubber, so popular on our beaches. In Vietnam and Korea everybody wears them even in winter; to a child coming to us from either country, the wearing of shoes spells both luxury and discomfort.

Unless you keep after him, your child will parade about the house and the yard barefoot; the conditioned reflex instilled in us in our youth that bare feet bring on head colds will make us pursue him with the demand that he put on something, any kind of slipper, sandal or cowboy boot.

If he is a boy, the boots are your best bet. The effeminate footwear of the movie cowboy has become, to adolescents all over the world, a symbol of virility and toughness. If your boy refuses to put on either sneakers or Start-Rite molded footwear, plonk him into a pair of cowboy boots from Sears Roebuck and let him loose. He may wince and mince his way to the neighbors', but that very night you will need force, not persuasion, to make him take them off before going to bed.

Girls are more discerning; the question of shoes is apt to be delicate if your daughter on her arrival is older than four. In the early stages, a visit to the shoe shop may turn into agony, as lack of language leaves her no means of communication other than facial expression. If she would only throw a tantrum, it would be preferable; a child who lies down on the floor, kicking and screaming, can be picked up and removed; although no shopkeeper or his attendant will love her for it, they will sympathize with your condition.

The facial expression of utter, regal disapproval is the more trying and effective torture. I have seen my wife, soon after the arrival of our elder daughter, brought to the verge of tears by a motionless little hunk of stolid disapprobation, surrounded by open boxes of dainty little shoes and two adults kneeling at her feet, pleading with her to try on this sweet little pair of oxbloods costing twenty dollars because of its orthopedic secrets. On that particular occasion the child had seen a pair of loafers on the feet of a neighboring girl whom she admired; she could not understand that they did not come in her size and the only way she could convey that she was prepared to wait for them till Doomsday was to freeze into a small immovable mass. The battle ended in a draw; ultimately she settled for a pair of lurid two-tone saddle shoes, black and white, which made her look like a participant in a floating crap game, but as they were all she was prepared to wear we had to swallow our snobbery. She was offered a balloon on a stick by the attendant, after we had paid our bill; she deigned to have it forced upon her and left the shop, dragging it behind her. It was the only time in my life I saw a child express martyrdom by means of a balloon.

Later we realized what our mistake had been. As in the case of the first breakfast, we had faced her with the responsibility of choosing from fifteen alternatives, which was thirteen more than she could cope with. The thing to do would have been not to take her with us to the shop at all, but for my wife to have brought home two pairs of shoes and let the child make up her mind, at her ease, which ones she preferred.

The loafers, by the way, are by no means forgotten; sometimes I suspect that her interest in her own growing process centers uniquely on the hidden dream of, one day, looking like the wonderful creature she saw walk past the house once, when she was very little.

19

Clothes

Boys aren't fussy, they don't mind what you put on them as long as it doesn't hamper their movements or make them look funny in the eyes of their peers. Girls are a different matter.

Never mind how young they are, to them a dress isn't just something you have to put on before you are allowed to burst out the front door into the open, it is something that either enhances or dims your natural charm and beauty. A social worker of my acquaintance, who has placed more unplaceable children than anyone else I know, always brings along a new dress when she has to take a little girl to her new home, a dark and frightening experience. I once accompanied her on one of those errands; the little girl was three years old, did not speak a word of English, and was going to a temporary home, prior to placement. To see the little thing come out the door, heading for the unknown, was a profoundly disturbing experience which left me shaken until I witnessed, in the car, the magic transformation of the child when the social worker opened a box with a new dress in it, held it out to her and asked, "Would you like to put that on now?" She must have spoken an international language of women, for the little girl, who technically could not have understood a word, knew instantly what she meant. She was so bewitched by the beautiful red velvet dress she was invited to put on that all the terror that had clouded her little face seemed to vanish and the tears that had been running down her cheeks stopped at once, although her body still shuddered occasionally with sobs. She was helped into the red dress professionally, and she seemed to put it on professionally—as if she had often spent hours observing herself critically in a long mirror, turning around, and around again, tugging at sleeves, patting a collar, to shake her head in the end and say with a disapproving scowl, "This doesn't do a *thing* for me."

The red velvet dress did a lot for her; when she finally stepped out of the car and bravely walked toward the future, she was ready to face whatever might be coming, convinced that people would say, "Look! Who is that pretty little girl coming up our driveway?"

Most of the conflicts my wife has had so far with our two daughters have been about clothes. For reasons incomprehensible to the male, some dresses are accepted with delight, put on in joyous anticipation and modeled proudly in the living room, with the studious nonchalance that seems to come naturally to all models; from that moment on, this is the dress she will want to wear on all the wrong occasions. Other dresses seem just as

charming and delightful, but the moment they are lifted
out of their bed of tissue paper and held up for scrutiny,
they provoke an ugly sound of derision and the infuriating words, "I don't like *that*." This is the moment that I,
as an outsider, find hardest to take. Who does she think
she is, to stand there three feet tall, hands on hips, nose
puckered as at an offensive smell, sticking out her tongue
at an absolutely darling little dress, lovingly chosen for
her by her mother after hours of agonizing reappraisal?

In the beginning this recurrent situation became a con-
test of wills. "Never mind whether you like it or not, *this*
is the dress you're going to wear to school tomorrow!
You look absolutely *darling* in it."

"I don't want to."

"Never mind what you want or don't want, this is the
dress you're going to wear and that's *final!*"

This dialogue was followed by the motionless stance
of gloom on the part of the child, and by soul-searching,
sighs and despondency in the parental bedroom later that
night.

In the end, we found a solution. Marjorie invested in a
collection of small cloth bunnies, poodles and pussy-cats
that could be sewn onto any dress and that came with a
variety of matching ribbons. Now, when a dress is received with the face that launched a thousand rows, Marjorie says, "Hmm, maybe you're right. It needs *something*. It's a little—I don't know—a little *dull*. It needs
something to bring out its character, something to make
it a little more dramatic. Let me see what I can do to-
night."

This patter, incomprehensible except to denizens of
the world of fashion, defuses the bomb before the fuse

has even been lit. That night a poodle is applied to the left breast, or a bunny to a front pocket, and a matching ribbon is sewn above the hem. The next morning, when the dress thus dramatized is modeled reluctantly and with profound suspicion in the living room, Daddy, who has been reading the newspaper, gasps with unbelief at the appearance of this vision of charm, elegance and beauty in the doorway. "My, where did you get that wonderful dress?" he cries, with the conviction of the villain in a farce. "How absolutely lovely! Mummy, where did you get this? When?"

I am fully aware that my days of deception are numbered, but while they last it works like a charm. The scowl of suspicion changes into the supercilious sneer of the cover girl, the slouched shoulders and ploddingly planted feet of dumb rebellion become the nonchalant stance of the fashion model; next thing we know, it has to be stripped off her, snarling and spitting, because she insists on wearing it to climb trees in or on an expedition with her current bosom friend in a rowboat.

Don't let any of this be cause for alarm. Only when the battle of the clothes is joined will you know that the cowed, deprived little refugee girl has been finally exorcised. When your daughter puckers her nose and sticks out her tongue for the first time at a dress her mother has chosen for her with love and indecision, by all means react as any father would. But realize at the same time, in the back of your mind, with a joy that may be hard to hide, that at last she is a normal little girl and no longer a wandering waif, flotsam of war.

20

Teeth

THE most common affliction among children from Asia is bad teeth. Their diet has been insufficient, dental care nonexistent, so most of them turn up with a miniature graveyard in their mouths which, when first revealed by an engaging smile, may fill you with dismay. Luckily, they arrive when they still have their milk teeth; if you get them to a dentist fast, chances are that the second lot will be all right. It is a wise assumption, however, that you will run into some heavy dentist's bills before your child can be considered up to our standards.

The dental work will involve a lot of drilling and probing, all of which is painful; it is best to take him to a children's dentist right away. Inquire among mothers in your neighborhood which dentist is "best with children," for you must be careful not to create an intense resistance in your child after the first visit. Teeth are likely to be his major problem for several years to come;

to have him throw a fit every time he is strapped down in a dentist's chair is something you, he and the dentist can do without. Otherwise, you will sit in the waiting room, listening to raucous shrieks, guttural sounds of strangulation and the dull drumming of heels; it is better to take him directly to a man who, out of a personal predilection that passes our understanding, has decided upon a career as a children's dentist. Your child will emerge from the treatment with a medal or a ring, and the grossest flattery of his courage is in order.

When the first teeth are shed, we found it good practice to perpetuate the hoary deception of the fairy who exchanges a tooth for a penny when she finds it in an envelope under the child's pillow at dead of night. By that time, the tooth will have come to stand for many a grim battle, and not to him alone. You will probably find that, after the fairy has removed it from under the pillow at the time of the midnight pot, he will stick the unsightly little object onto a card with a piece of Scotch tape, mark it "Johnny's first tooth" and put it with his documents, in the strongbox.

21

Play

BASICALLY, all children's play falls into two categories. It is either a retreat into a world of imagination inaccessible to adults, or the externalization of exuberance in which adults are welcome as chasers, ball-throwers or means of conveyance, such as a horse.

You may find that your child's play, after the initial bashfulness has been overcome, fits into the second category. In that case, you will soon see him running with the neighborhood children, trying to join in their games. The world of other children is familiar to him; this is the type of play that is universal. Children from Asia who fit into the first category are a different matter. In their case, the secret world of childhood is even more inaccessible to adults than it normally is. They probably have known very few toys; if they come from an orphanage in Vietnam, it is certain that they have known none at all. All they will have had to aid their imagination was their own power of evocation.

There are children who don't have this power; they are the ones who have sat about for hours on end in hot, reeking orphanage yards, surrounded by hundreds of their kind, vacantly whiling the hours away in the sun, too emotionally deprived to realize that what they were experiencing was boredom. To teach such a child to play is difficult enough; if, at the same time, he is inebriated by the heady nectar of your affection, of which he never seems to get enough, the task becomes doubly difficult. The mere fact of your physical presence is so important to him that anything which may help keep you there will be instantly forthcoming. If he feels that by making ritual movements with blocks or throwing rings at a stick he can keep you with him, he'll do so with a zest that may lead you to believe he is delighted with the new game. But when you get up and try to sneak out, assuming him to be absorbed in it, he will instantly drop it and follow you wherever you may go, to kick up a storm when at a given moment you insist upon privacy.

This will change, but it will take longer than you expected and may take longer than you can bear. In that case, there is only one way out: other children—and even they may not work until his first thirst for affection has been slaked. If you can find a family with children his age, preferably children of his own background, you will be allowed to sit chatting on the periphery with their mother; you may even be allowed to go to the bathroom, on condition you announce your destination clearly.

No one can say how long this stage will last or when your child will begin actually to play rather than pretend to do so as the price for your presence. The day will come when some game, some coloring book, some set of building blocks will suddenly absorb him to a point where, for a few minutes at least, he can exist without the reassurance of your presence. You may conclude that, at last, you have found a toy that suits him; but in reality you have given him the beginnings of a sense of security: if you go away, this no longer necessarily means that you will never come back. It will take a long time before his trust is complete.

The children who from the moment they arrive show a marvelous capacity for keeping themselves amused are the ones who give the greatest cause for concern. Not because they may come to grief, but because the image they present, sometimes for many months, has little to do with their true selves. They are the ones social workers refer to as "duck soup," compared to others who are more demanding. They seem completely relaxed and at ease; their pleasant behavior is obviously not the outcome of training or drill, they seem naturally placid and easygoing. They will accompany you to beauty salon or kaffee klatsch and present no problems; all you need do is give them a book, settle them in a corner and they'll sit there for hours on end, just leafing through it, maybe quietly talking to themselves; when they have finished the book they will start all over again. At home, a child like this will play with a toy train or teddy bear, maybe dress up and play different roles to himself; a girl will be happy with a doll, a doll's pram and a doll's bed with some scraps of material; they will keep her occupied for as long as you want. You will conclude that this child has adapted beautifully, that, in her case, at least, you have nothing to worry about.

Maybe you haven't, but one thing is certain: the little angel, so serenely floating along with you and your family, is not the real child. The real child lives elsewhere, in a land you will never know; a land where complete security reigns, beyond the reach of violence or tenderness, sorrow or joy. The secret of his equanimity and pleasant behavior is that he is simply not there, not really; at best he is a visitor to your home who, sensibly, won't rock the boat but amicably adjust to any demands put upon him in the certain knowledge that it is all impermanent anyhow. Tomorrow or the next day he'll be off to some other home, some other Mummy and Daddy, some other dog, pussy, kitchen and yard; he doesn't fight, cling, weep or simper because nothing touches him much.

These children are more severely damaged emotionally than their obviously disturbed brothers and sisters, who present their new parents with a more immediate challenge. It will take a considerable time before they finally and quite suddenly move out of their secret world into yours. When that happens, you are in for a surprise, and it is not likely to be a pleasant one. Suddenly, the little harmless butterfly will reverse the laws of nature by turning into a caterpillar. All at once, quickly enough to warrant the word surprise, the child will become as demanding, moody, jealous and afflicted by the insatiable need for affection as the others once were, who by then will have become normal children with the problems and idiosyncrasies typical of their age.

No one can say exactly what brings about the transformation. Nobody knows what finally tips the scales between gregariousness and suspicion. One thing is certain: he'll give you a run for your money that will leave you limp and exhausted, aghast at your own lack of patience. It is much easier to cope with a child who arrives with all the abrasive symptoms of insecurity and emotional neglect—at least you know from the start what you are faced with. This is different, something like a betrayal, a breach of confidence. You will begin by searching for something you have done or omitted to do that will explain the enigma of your reasonable, easygoing child suddenly turning into a fiend, snarling and malevolent one moment, cloying and whining for affection the next. When you can find no reason for his behavior, you may feel outraged; the sudden strain upon your emotional resources may make you intemperate in your reaction.

There are no hard and fast rules as to how to cope with this situation; each of us will have to find his or her own way of bringing it under control. One thing should not be forgotten in the face of those horrible moods, those groundless tears, that equally groundless laughter: if you had not done such a good job so far, if you had not ultimately worn down his defenses and made him accept you as his parent, he would not now be kicking your shins while clutching your thighs, daring you, taunting you, begging you to give him back his peace of mind by rejecting him and thus allowing him to retreat once more into that secret country where he was so happy, at peace with himself and the world. What you have done, in fact, is to coax him back to life.

If he challenges you to a conflict, don't let it worry you. If, despite your good intentions and resolutions, he gets what he asks for, with knobs on, don't feel guilty. Make sure that, once you are both worn and wan after the battle of the day, you give him what he really came for: lots of love and tenderness. He is no different from other children, only it took him a little while longer to believe that, at last, he has found his home.

22

Jealousy

JEALOUSY is not an exclusively human vice. Anyone who ever had two dogs or a dog and a cat will know that animals can be just as jealous as humans. If you pat one dog, you have to pat the other; if you are taking a sand-spur out of the paw of one, the other will start limping. Considering that jealousy is a natural instinct rather than human depravity, it should not be taken too seriously. But these children may show it with a disturbing inten-sity, particularly during the first few months after their arrival.

This problem is especially acute if you receive two children at the same time, as we did. Whether the child arrives in the company of his own brother or sister or finds one ready-made in his new home, however, the problem will be much the same.

What lies at the bottom of the sometimes almost insane jealousy of some of our Asian children? After the traumatic experience of a total severance not only from their family and their country but from their own previous selves, their overriding emotion is one of insecurity. Although they will be at pains not to make it obvious, the moment they set eyes on us they secretly reach out to us with desperate intensity. They understand a great deal more of what goes on around them than we assume, even though they do not speak our language. They knew at once that the stewardess on the plane and the woman who escorted their convoy, though kind and nice, were not there to stay. Even without the extensive preparation by photographs and descriptions of their future home, they know, the moment they set eyes on us: "Here are two people who will stay with me if only I can make them." But "them" will soon change into "her." Important as the father may be, in the beginning the mother is the center of the child's life, the pivot around which all his thoughts and actions will revolve until he feels secure enough to branch out.

It is unlikely that you will notice any jealousy in him immediately after his arrival. Some children show it within a few days; others take months. The fact is that before he will express jealousy openly the child has to feel at least partially secure, secure enough to risk his mother's disapproval. During the initial period he will be at pains to show only his best side, or what he has come to believe to be his best. Yet, underneath it all he will see the other children in your home as his competitors for the basic necessities of life: food, clothing and, above all, affection. This will soon give rise to violent arguments, which, unless you clearly understand what is happening, may lead you to conclusions about his character and disposition that are unfair. Any child, even one who eventually proves to be easy-going and generous, may appear during those first months to be a spiteful, violent curse from the East, the most catastrophic mistake you ever made.

How do you cope with this? Do you give him preference over your other children, not to mention your dog and your husband? The answer is yes. This is why it is so important, if you have children of your own, to discuss the adoption with them beforehand and to explain to them that when the child arrives he is likely to be difficult and unpleasant, hard to get along with. Only when you have managed to make him believe that he is a full and permanent member of your family and that "love" is not diminished by distribution, will his jealousy be reduced to normal proportions and most of his unhappy characteristics disappear.

So, roll with the punches, indulge him as much as you can, especially in the beginning, and don't try to explain to him other people's rights and prerogatives before he at least understands what you are saying. You cannot express in sign language the reasonable demand that he must respect other people's rights—only things like "no," "come here" and "you are my child," the latter by hugging him and saying those words very close to him while his dark, anguished eyes read them off your lips; they will probably be the first words in his new language he will understand.

How long will it last, this ordeal? For an ordeal it is. Your other children, however sincere in their intentions and initial patience, will be unable to keep it up. The span of their altruism is limited; they will soon revert to their naturally egocentric selves and show a distressing disregard for the emotional problems of their new brother. They will snarl and hiss and slap and kick with the same abandon as he; even the dog may join in the general melee, until you will have the feeling that your family, once so happy and united in mutual affection, has turned into a drunk tank in the county jail.

All I can say to cheer you is that it is temporary. Sooner or later the moment will come when he will feel sure enough of your affection to let up a little and give the other members of the litter a chance to drink. The first sign of the changing tide may be given by the dog. He has been jealous too; even if he has always been good with children, he will at first have glowered and growled at the newcomer. When, at last, he allows himself to be petted and given a cookie, you are over the hump. Any moment now his tail will start wagging and soon thereafter your new son, new no longer, will, for the first time, give a toy to his brother.

To get him there is the woman's job, and when the awful qualms of the onset of depression tighten your stomach, remember that things are not so different after all. You carried the others under your heart, him on your hip. That, really, is what it amounts to: for him to become your son and you to become his mother you have to go through another pregnancy, and not a pre-adoptive one this time.

23

Sex

IF YOUR new child is under two years old, he will develop like any child of that age as far as the discovery and uses of sex are concerned. Should he come to you between the ages of three and six, you may be in for a few jolts.

Most of our children, before they entered the orphanage, grew up in a situation where sex was not only freely discussed but on occasion observed in action. Asian families of modest means live in one room, where they sleep on the floor; this gives the children a specialized knowledge far in advance of their age and in some cases a precocious bawdiness which, before they have learned our language, is communicated by gesture or drawing. I know of one staid young couple who were horrified when their charming little boy, so gay and endearing, whom they sent waltzing to kindergarten like a little angel in blue jeans, was cannonballed back by the school because he drew, in the artistic free-for-all called "creative play," manikins with enormous erections chasing stumbling motherkins with pendulous breasts and hirsute figleaves. They were further disturbed by beady black eyes greedily observing their two innocent little girls at bathtime; the result was that they depicted the child to the social worker who had placed him as a monster of depravity who had to be removed before he was given a chance to pervert an innocent family.

Most parents of Asian children over the age of three have had moments in which their first impulse was to recoil from what, to our peculiar morality, presents itself as rank obscenity. Some of us coped with the situation calmly and with understanding, others merely muddled through, yet others found cause for severe reprimand, even corporal punishment. We should not exaggerate the lasting effect of any one of these reactions. Whether we treat our children with the wisdom of identification, try to back out of the situation with all the symptoms of moral cowardice or bang them like gongs, it doesn't matter much as long as they are made to understand that while we may be angry at the gesture or drawing, it does not make any difference in our feelings toward them.

What is amazing and impressive about our children, I think, is the miracle of their innocence after all they have seen, heard and gone through. Even the child who drew the satyr chasing the nymph did so in total innocence, as far as the sin of fornication is concerned. If a boy can draw a horse absent-mindedly dangling a fire hose while it grazes, without being dragged in front of the juvenile court of Daddy's outraged sense of propriety, then a child who has at some time during his short and harsh life

witnessed the act of procreation and in fundamental innocence draws what he saw must not be judged as if his
intention were to sell his artistry for its prurient interest to tourists in the French Quarter of New Orleans.
The mother who spanked the little boy and called the
agency with the request that the bad fruit be removed
must have had a pretty cross-eyed concept of the basic
virtues of man, the least of which is his sense of propriety. The child was, luckily, placed with another family
that was less strait-laced; after a few trial runs obviously
intended to gauge the reaction, which was negative, he
began to draw the pussy-cats, flowers and grinning suns
that were more gratifyingly rewarded, and, to my
knowledge, he never returned to his old specialty.

So, unless you are in the habit of chasing your wife
stark naked down the corridor with the outward sign of
a successful marriage, the subject of your child's art will
rapidly change. Should there be little boys in your family, or little girls, as the case may be, your new child's
obvious familiarity with the anatomical differences between the sexes should be welcomed, casually, as an asset
rather than as a perversity. Toymakers have, tentatively,
begun to manufacture dolls with cute little plastic geni-
talia, thus far at a price of nearly thirty dollars, which
must be the price of progress. Your child, at least, will
not need this expensive initiation into the facts of life; he
knows them, he takes them for granted and they won't
bother him as long as you take care not to show that they
bother you.

Apart from all this, how *does* one deal at a moment's
notice with this precocious knowledge which is bound to
startle us when we least expect it? One early morning

our youngest was playing on our bed for a few minutes prior to being whisked through the potting, washing, dressing, combing and breakfast routine. Suddenly, out of the pristine blue, I heard the child say, "This is what boys have." I peered over my glasses from behind my newspaper and saw that she was fingering, pensively, the tassel on a little ornamental pillow. Marjorie, who was reading the woman's page while I grimly scanned the editorials, said, "You don't say."

"Yes," continued the four-year-old. "I saw it. I saw one boy take down his pants."

"Fancy that," Marjorie said.

The reaction, or rather the lack of it, seemed to disappoint the child. "I saw two," she said. "I saw three. I saw nine, five, four. I saw a—a hunnerd!"

"Gee," Marjorie said, turning the page, "girl, that's living."

It was the moment I decided to let the women in my life work out their sex education among themselves.

24

Prayers

EXCEPT to those among you for whom praying is a daily conversation with a familiar and ever present God, to teach a child of four to say grace at table and a child's prayer at bedtime may seem an anachronism. To make these children, victims of war, jetsam of man's inhumanity to man, go down on their knees at night, fold their hands and pray to "gentle Jesus, meek and mild" may seem as sacrilegious as to teach a dog to refuse a cookie when it is said to come from the Devil but to make him snatch it the moment it is said to come from Jesus.

A spinster cousin of my father's had such a dog. She lived, fifty years ago, in a courtyard behind one of Amsterdam's canals in a little two-room house, part of a retirement home for Christian women built in 1672. She also had a canary which sang to the accompaniment of a harmonium as if it knew the words of the hymn, and a cat that was made to pray every night for the poor pus-

sies in Africa and China. As a child, I loved visiting
Cousin Marie because she baked special cookies that,
after being buttered and sprinkled with chocolate chips,
tasted as no cookies have ever tasted since. I saw nothing
odd in her religious menagerie; at that age it had not yet
occurred to me that animals are not included in the
Christian precept for salvation. Cousin Marie was convinced that Jesus had had a dog that followed Him
everywhere, picked up the scraps from the feeding of the
multitude on the shores of the Sea of Galilee, sat behind
His chair at the Last Supper and waited faithfully by his
Master's grave, certain of His resurrection. In later years
I came to consider Cousin Marie with the sophistication,
bordering on condescension, of spiritual maturity. But
since the two little children have come into our home,
I have begun to think of her in the same terms as the
little boy who was ready to suffer religion if it was the
price for those delicious cookies. Fifty years later I still
remember the atmosphere in the poky little house with
its Dutch door, the top half of which was always open,
overlooking a courtyard with pump, old elm trees and
red brick paths bordered by hedges shorn like lambs in
the fall. I remember the atmosphere of kindness and
goodness which did not jar with her shrewd and unsentimental appraisal of others. There was about her calm,
massive person a feeling of security, a mixture of fairness
and understanding which, combined with her simple un-
dogmatic faith, made her little house seem more like a
home than my own, where the atmosphere crackled with
intellectual excitement and where no animals were allowed.

I don't believe we can hope to resurrect in our house

that serenity, that calm, uncompromising kindness; it all seems part of the canary trilling "How Great Thou Art," the little dog resisting the temptation of the Devil and the pussy-cat praying for her heathen brothers and sisters in Africa. But remembering Cousin Marie made me realize that whatever I may think myself about prayer at this time of my life will be meaningless to a child of four living in a world peopled with toys, dogs, a kitty and two kindly giants whose lair he shares.

We begin our meals by saying grace, Quaker fashion: the family holding hands around the table and sitting silently for a minute or so, eyes closed in private prayer. But it doesn't really matter what form the prayer takes, as long as it comes naturally to you; to start saying grace solely for the sake of the children, while you yourself sit there with the pursed mouth of the age of doubt, is not a good idea. Even if you are an agnostic, there is no harm in reflecting for a few minutes every day upon the mystery that underlies our lives. What was it that brought the four of us together as we sit there at our table, heads bent, hands folded, in silence? Very little of it was our own doing. Here am I, who once rode a tricycle down the garden path, irresistibly tempted by the forbidden world beyond the gate, and look at me now: the parent of two little waifs from Asia, grains of sand from among the millions on a distant beach. How did they get here? What power, what destiny made them, who once squalled in the arms of an unknown woman half a world away, end up at our table? What intricate chain of cause and effect, how many accidents, twists of fate, brief encounters, lucky stars and missed chances led them here, to look up with a smile after my "Amen" and call me

"Dad"? Anyone who sits down at table with children like ours will not violate his intellectual integrity if he joins hands and bends his head for a moment of silent reflection on the vast, mysterious forces that propel us.

At night, when the children kneel by their bedside to pray in those old and by now mawkish terms of meekness, mildness and kindness to others, we may, as we sit there, be troubled by uneasy thoughts about Sigmund Freud, Auschwitz, or the satanic cruelty of man that slammed a crown of thorns on the little heads now bent at our knee. But rather than sow our own doubt, sorrow and confusion in the freshly plowed soil of their young lives, we should give them the chance to discover in our home, touched by their very arrival by a magic wand of kindness and joy, their own little courtyard with old elm trees and red brick paths bordered by hedges shorn like lambs in the fall. It does not matter what we think, or think we ought to think; it does not matter what our intellectual interpretation of what happened is. We have, whether we like it or not, put into practice the essential teaching of the mystics of all religions; and even if a God of love should be an illusion, we have no right to denounce to our children at this tender age the perennial principle underlying our troubled and self-conscious practice.

25

The First Crisis

ACTUALLY, the title of this chapter should be *"my* first crisis"; it is unlikely that many parents will find themselves in a similar situation. But there will be a first crisis, sometime, and you may discover that your Asian child will react in the same way ours did.

A few weeks after the arrival of the two little girls, Marjorie, who had not been feeling well for a month or so, was struck out of the blue with such excruciating pain that she could hardly bear it. She was rushed to a hospital and underwent major surgery the next day. When the first frenzied emergency was over, I found myself, dazed and groggy with fatigue, with two children on my hands whose new mother of a few weeks would not be back for a month. It was hard luck that they should be struck this blow so soon after their arrival; they had hardly been given a chance to get accustomed to Marjorie before she was whisked off, at dead of night, with all the ominous symptoms of disaster.

Once I knew that she was going to be all right, I decided to do what I could to diminish the impact of this emotional shock on the children, who at the time spoke so little English that it was hard to make out how much they understood. Several of our women friends were eager to help, but I felt it would be wrong to confront the children with yet another female whom they would call Mummy. It would be tricky and probably end up as a mess, but I was determined to look after them single-handed, with no other help than the kind Negro maid who came in every morning and with whom they were familiar. We would telephone Marjorie twice a day and I would take them along when I went to visit her; we would do everything we could to keep up the illusion of being a family, although up to that time we had been merely four people living under the same roof, in the process of establishing some kind of relationship.

Two days after I started my experiment in housekeeping, it looked as if we were going to make it. That night, after I had given the children their supper, I let the dogs out and started the bath. The two days had been hectic and at times I had felt like a juggler with seven hot plates in the air, but as I knelt beside the bath, soaping the two thin little bodies, I congratulated myself on my mastery of the situation.

Suddenly, I realized that I had left the dogs outside. It was midwinter, the temperature ten degrees, the pampered old mutts should not be left out in the cold. I told the children, in pidgin English accompanied by sign language, to go on washing themselves while I went downstairs to let the woof-woofs in. I raced down the stairs, opened the front door, took a deep breath to whistle, but the dogs stormed in and I was overwhelmed by such a stupendous stench that my first thought was that there must have been a gas attack of some sort, or maybe a tank truck had been struck by a train at the railroad crossing and spilled poisonous fumes down the road. But after I hurriedly closed the door the stench did not seem to diminish—quite the reverse. I staggered back into the hall, gasping for breath, and saw the younger of the two dogs reeling about as if he were drunk, slavering at the mouth, tears streaming down his snout, while the other sat panting in a corner in a state of collapse, with a pink display of overweight stomach and multiple pendulous breasts. Then the answer struck me: it was they who had brought in the stench, they had been in a fight with a skunk. The potency of the odor, now rapidly spreading through the entire house, was such that something had to be done at once. I could not let them out into the cold again; already they sat there shivering, teeth chattering, on the verge of pneumonia.

As I stood there, at a loss to know what to do, two naked little girls appeared at the top of the stairs, giggling, asking, "Daddy, wadda woof-woof?" They were dripping wet; the house was cold, they too were in imminent danger of catching pneumonia. I don't know what I answered; I remember the words "woof-woof" and "stinky-stinky" followed by the admonition that they should get back into their bath, quick! But there they stood, at the top of the stairs, their faces puckered in disgust, expressing nausea with a highly evocative sound while sticking out their tongues.

I shooed them back into the bathroom with a sudden

burst of Dutch vituperation that made them scurry out of sight like mice; then, reeling, I fought my way to the kitchen through the giddying whorls of stench emanating from the gasping dogs against the wall, grabbed the telephone directory, looked up "Veterinarians" in the yellow pages, and dialed the first home number listed. The telephone rang for some time before a gruff male voice answered, saying, "Yes?" I explained to him that I was sorry to disturb him at this hour but that I suddenly found myself faced with an emergency: my two old dogs had just been hit by a skunk, smack between the eyes, and now lay about in the hall in a coma, poisoning the whole house, while my two little children sat shivering in the bath and my wife was in the hospital. Please, please, Doctor, what should I do?

"Do?" the gruff voice asked, with obvious distaste.

"I must do something!" I cried, the vise of hysteria tightening around my stomach. "What can I do to get rid of this stench?"

There was a silence that seemed to last a long time. Looking back on the episode later and trying to explain what followed, I made an effort to identify with the man: sitting down in front of his television set after a busy day at the clinic, with his shoes off at last and his belt unbuckled; just as he was lifting his weary legs onto the ottoman, there went the telephone and some nut started to yell for free advice. Doctor, Doctor, my wife is in the hospital, my kids are in the bath, and my dogs have been hit by a skunk. Seen from that chair, that weariness after a long day of spaying people's poodles, castrating their tomcats and performing a hysterectomy on somebody's pet rabbit, he seemed justified in saying what he said:

"Why don't you try washing them down with tomato juice?"

"Tomato juice . . . ?" I repeated, incredulously.

"Sure. Wash 'em down with tomato juice, and see what happens."

"How—how much tomato juice per dog, Doctor?" I stammered, bewildered by the bizarre advice, but ready to go through with it—anything to get rid of the odor which by now must have reached the attic.

"Oh, about a quart," he answered. "Pour it in a bucket and slop it on 'em. It's sure to have *some* effect."

"All right—okay—thank you, Doctor," I said gratefully. I put the phone down and, holding my breath, grabbed both dogs by their collars and dragged them through the kitchen into the laundry. Later I visualized the doctor lifting his legs onto the ottoman with satisfaction; and I reflected that it must be rare for a veterinarian to be given a chance of getting even with one of the freeloaders who pick his brains by telephone without ever paying a cent. He seemed to have risen to the occasion.

The moment I had locked the dogs in the laundry I staggered back upstairs to put the children to bed. I found that they were already in the process of going there of their own accord; I was received by two wrinkled noses and again that highly expressive elemental sound of nausea. Whatever other talents these children might turn out to have, they certainly had a gift for the drama. "You go bye-byes," I said in what must have been, by then, a falsetto. "Bye-byes, bye-byes, both of you, while I go downstairs: soapy-soapy!" I rubbed my chest with both hands. "Soapy-soapy, woof-woof!"

They must have thought I was debilitated or intoxicated, babbling distraught baby language to two tough, battle-scarred orphans who had lived by their wits in the postwar jungle of a Korean city for the better part of their lives. But at that point I was not conscious of any incongruity; all I could see was the whole fragile edifice of illusions about Daddy, gamely coping single-handed with two toddlers, collapsing ignominiously under the impact of a smell.

The smell was really something. Months later some areas of the house still reeked of skunk; even now, more than a year later, despite countless shampoos, dippings and a small fortune in deodorant sprays, the dogs still smell of skunk if the weather is humid; they probably will go on doing so until the grave.

When I opened the door of the laundry again, it nearly knocked me out; the dogs, weeping, reeling, welcomed me with groundless trust. I found two quarts of tomato juice, pierced the lids and poured the contents into a bucket; after spreading some newspapers on the floor in a halfhearted gesture of competence I started to douse the poor numbskulls with it. It took time, but when I was through with them there wasn't a drop of tomato juice left in the bucket; all of it had been absorbed by their fur. To which extent this was so I discovered when one of them got away, staggered into the kitchen and shook himself vigorously. The result nearly made me burst into tears; all it took was one good shake by a dog soaked in tomato juice and we had a pop-art kitchen.

Suddenly the whole thing seemed such a nightmare that all I could think of was to call up the veterinarian again. I expected him to be even less forthcoming the second time than he had been the first, but something in my voice must have made him relent; to my question, "What do I do next? Do I let it dry on them?" he replied almost kindly, "Hell, no. If you do that you'll never get it out again; take 'em into the garden, hose 'em down."

"But, Doctor," I said, "I can't do that! They are ten years old, they're wet and it is ten degrees outside!"

"All right," he replied, calmly. "Then take them to the bathroom and rinse them under the shower."

I took them to the guest bathroom, Marjorie's pride, replete with miniature hand towels, a dainty powder box for the ladies, and a toilet seat covered with white fur; I took them there because it was the only bath that had a hand shower. I lifted them into the tub, turned on the water; as I started to hose them down, it looked as if blood came running out of their hides. Then the soggy fur of the long-haired one clogged the exhaust of the bath and there I was, on my knees in a bathroom that now looked like a butcher shop, with a bath full of blood in which grisly bits of fur were floating and two shivering dogs, still smelling overpoweringly of skunk.

I was so desperate to get the stench under control that I did something drastic. Years before, a generous friend of ours, whose firm imported French perfume, had sent me as a Christmas present a spray bomb of toilet water for the rugged male, called "Jenghiz Khan." I had used it once, and that was all; Marjorie had told me that if I used that stuff again she would leave me. Since then I had tried several times to donate it to other friends, but without success; they all took one whiff and put it down again, ready for the next man. Deluded by the adage that it takes a smell to kill a smell, I proceeded to spray the dogs with the toilet water for rugged males. I did more than spray them; I soaked them with it, rubbing their fur against the grain to make sure it got to the skin. It took me half an hour; then I gave up. The perfume had no effect whatsoever on the stench it was meant to exorcise; the two smells merely existed independently, one alongside the other. I dragged myself into the sitting room and collapsed in my chair, followed after a while by two pink dogs, reeking in equal parts of skunk and Jenghiz Khan.

Telling it like this, I must give the impression that it was a lark; at that moment, I could not discover a shimmer of humor in the situation. I was defeated, this was the end. I had failed on all fronts; the children were a mess, the house was a shambles, Marjorie desperately ill —how, dear God, would I ever get out of this?

As I sat there, at the deepest point of dejection, I suddenly became aware of a presence in the doorway to the passage and looked up. It was the older of my two new daughters.

"What are you doing here?" I asked. "Where are your slippers?" It was the first time I had spoken to her normally, not in the preposterous baby-pidgin I had thus far assumed to be appropriate.

She came into the room without a word, hoisted herself onto my lap and put her head on my shoulder. It was the first time she had done this; so far she had always shrunk from any physical contact. It was as if, struck by adversity, she had instinctively sought my comforting presence.

I don't know how long we sat there like that, but she soon fell asleep. When finally I carried her up to her bedroom, careful not to wake her, and put her down in her bed, far away from all she had ever known and loved, I felt confident and full of hope. A little light-headed, maybe, but calm and serene. For the first time since the children's arrival I felt like a father.

Two

Settling Down

26

Fellow Parents

AFTER your child has been with you awhile, you will probably be asked to join a group of parents who received their offspring through the same agency as you. As a rule, these groups get together once a year for a reunion and most of them publish a news-letter. There is one nationwide organization of adoptive parents that publishes a monthly called *Adoptalk;* but, excellent though it is, you will only on rare occasions find in it the advice we need in our specific situation as parents of Asian children. The reason why, in our case, I recommend you join the group is that, apart from the comfort it gives us to know that we are not the only couple of oddballs in our community, there will be occasions when older parents of Asian children might cite from their experience the solution to a problem which we, as novices, may have considered insurmountable.

But there is another reason why you should join the

group, and it may well be the most important one. Interracial adoptions are by no means fully accepted yet;
communal acceptance may be virtually complete, but
some local welfare agencies and government officials who
rule on these matters are not yet convinced that the
adoption of Asian children by Caucasian parents is a
sound idea. Their arguments against interracial adoptions
are based on insufficient evidence; the only ones who can
provide the evidence are adoptive parents like ourselves.
Your joining the group may well help to save more children like our own from misery, deprivation and, in some
cases, death.

So, even if you are a fanatical non-joiner like myself,
here is one instance where I say: join.

27

Relatives

SOME of you may be fortunate enough to belong to a family of saints; but even those happy few would do well to reflect for a moment upon the instinctive reaction of the human animal when an interloper invades the exclusive unit of the tribe.

The most civilized concept of adoption was probably held by the Romans in the later stages of the Empire. They not only equated adoption legally with blood affiliation, they frequently adopted mature men in recognition of their services, to grant them citizenship. There is, to my knowledge, no recorded instance in Roman history where, when the chips were down, the fact that a man was an adopted son rather than a natural one played a significant role in the reactions of his family. When, after the fall of the Roman Empire, Christianity took over the reins of civilization, adoption rapidly became so unpopular that adopted sons were occasionally referred to as "bastards" to keep up the pretense that they were natural sons of their adoptive father, born out of wedlock. This despite the frequent references to adoption in the New Testament where Christ and later His Apostles refer to the convert as "adopted by his Heavenly Father."

The long, uphill road to the emotional acceptance of the adopted child by the clan shows many hairpin bends of regression; even we have not arrived yet at the civilized concept of adoption held by the citizens of the Roman Empire. Quakers, for instance, despite their firm adherence to the principles and attitudes of early Christianity, cannot help falling victim occasionally to the tribal instinct, the sworn emotional enemy of adoption. One venerable family recently published a genealogy in which the names of the adopted members had been included only at the last moment, in response to the vociferous protests of the younger generation. Even so, their names were marked with an asterisk.

There can be no doubt that, enlightened and sophisticated as we may consider ourselves to be, we are still subject, below the threshold of our consciousness, to the ancient tribal reverence for the tie of blood. Most adoptive parents agree, once they let their hair down, that they had a much easier time with their relatives when they announced they were adopting a girl than if it had been a boy. In the sacramental myth of the tie of blood the male heirs carry on the line, the female offspring is of secondary importance. It may be that the established preference of adoptive parents for girls over boys has as its source this ancient tribal shibboleth; in any case, you should be prepared, despite reassurances to the contrary on the part of your family, for a deep-seated discomfort amounting to reluctance.

This reaction, prevalent among relatives in the case of any adoption, is markedly increased in our situation, especially in societies that have known some form of racial discrimination in the recent past. In Europe these are the ex-colonial nations, in the United States it is the Deep South. In Europe the Asian child has, apart from the ancestral sanctity of the tie of blood, the stigma of social inferiority to overcome; although the colonial empires of the last three centuries largely belong to the past, their prejudices and tabus survive, at least among the older generation. Human nature being what it is, the resistance to the adoption of an Asian child will be strongest in those families that have, at some time in the safely buried past, been "tainted" with Asian blood.

All I can say to comfort fellow parents and their children is that, by now, this prehistoric attitude has outlived its dignity and become ludicrous in the eyes of the younger generation. By the time our children are adults, chances are that the last vestiges of this particular sin of our fathers will have disappeared from our community. But some of it survives in our parents, perhaps even in ourselves although we may not be aware of it. I was by no means free of it myself when, as a young and eager sailor, I went about the world sowing my Quaker oats. During one lengthy tour of duty around the Malay Archipelago as the young mate of an ocean-going tugboat I recoiled, aghast, from the suggestion of marriage made by a charming Chinese girl from whom until that moment I had anything but recoiled. It was not just the normal young man's wallaby leap at the mere mention of wedlock; the idea of marrying a person of a different race filled me with confusion and embarrassment. It wasn't done, in those last days of the Dutch colonial empire; anyone who turned up in our pre-war society with an Asian bride was considered a coward and a weakling and was ostracized for sullying the purity of our tribal blood.

I mention this because I am convinced that all members of my generation, including Americans, carry a remnant of discrimination in their subconscious for the simple reason that it was part of the general mores of the society in which we grew up. It is nothing to be ashamed of; if anything, it should make us lenient toward those of our relatives who view with ill-concealed dismay the prospect of our adopting an Asian child. They may sincerely want to approve of everything we do, and objectively they do approve, but subjectively they suffer.

How do we cope with their unhappy bewilderment? The best solution, I have found, is not to cope at all. Like all prejudices, racial discrimination, even in its most discreet and self-conscious form, is concerned with symbols, not individuals. The gentle Quakers who insisted, with friendly doggedness, on marking adopted children with an asterisk did so as a service to truth, not as an insult to their unknown nephews and nieces. Their sin was not the marking with the asterisk, but the implication of second-class status within their family structure. Once we have arrived at the civilized concept of adoption the Romans held, the asterisks in the genealogy will merely provide interesting additional information on the people concerned.

Until that day, we'll have to leave it to our adopted

children to do their own civilizing of reluctant relatives. They will make a fast and thorough job of it, once they have been given a chance to zero in on Granddad. Not only are they irresistibly appealing as individuals, they have an innate respect for old age and a sincere yearning to belong to a family—a yearning at least as ineradicable and instinctive as our veneration of the tie of blood. No grandfather can long resist the passionate desire of this sudden, ready-made grandchild to belong to him, to love him and honor him; the general consensus among adoptive parents is that the dourest grandfathers make the earliest converts. After that, the conquest of the family tree is merely a matter of time; in most parents' experience the children's grandparents fall first, the uncles last.

As to the children's contemporaries, they have a whole new set of prejudices, but racial discrimination is not one of them. All that's needed, really, is for us dodos to die out—until then the best we can do is be kind to the helpless, including ourselves.

28

Pets

You will probably have heard of cases where, after the arrival of a child in a family, the household pets had a very difficult time adjusting. Animals are extremely jealous; being purely instinctive creatures, it takes them a while to realize that they will have to put up or get out.

In the case of your child, the crisis in the lives of your cat and your dog will be even more pronounced. A baby, at least to start with, is merely a squalling, smelly presence in a basket four feet off the floor over which the parents bend with drooling delight. An Asian child arriving in the house presents, even at the youngest age at which these children come over, immediate and active competition.

Marjorie and I had discussed the possible reactions of our two old mutts to the arrival of the children in our family; we were not prepared for the canine tragedy that followed. One dog was ten years old, the other seven;

they had accompanied us on many voyages by ship, even
by air. The elder of them, at the age of five months, had
jumped through a porthole of our ship in New Orleans
during a thunderstorm and bounced onto the expanse
of my sleeping stomach, with the result that animal and
captain, screaming with fright, discovered each other in
opposite corners of the cabin after I had finally found
the light switch. At first we vainly tried to give the animal away, as we already had a dog; she turned into one
of the wiliest, most engaging and at times most infuriating of devious, lazy bitches. The next one we picked up
from the shelter of the Humane Society in Fort Myers,
Florida, after our original ship's dog had died, leaving the
little bitch from New Orleans crushed with grief, vainly
crying with a plaintive sound that disturbed us to the
point where we set out, four men strong, to find a substitute. He was a male of about five months, pretty to look
at but, as the keeper of the shelter warned us, with a
fiendish appetite for human calves, especially those of
preachers. As we had no preachers on board ship, or so I
believed with the lack of self-knowledge typical of au-
thors, we carried the pretty dog back on board in tri-
umph and presented him to the bereaved little mutt who
refused to acknowledge his presence for the better part
of a year. But at least it stopped the whining, which had
been so persistent and so feminine that every single man
on board had been helpless under its gentle ministrations.

It was this ill-assorted, ill-tempered, overfed, overpam-
pered pair of animals that suddenly found themselves
confronted by two little girls with whom there was
never even any question of competition. Until the arrival
of the children they had lived in a world where shoes, hose

and trouser legs led up to welcome laps on which to put their sentimental heads, with one weather eye open for the cookies on the tea tray; now there were only shoes and, occasionally, a small unfamiliar face peering, upside down, underneath the coffee table.

Both dogs began by growling; after it had been made clear to them, first in theory, then in practice, that they had to shut up or be exiled, the sly little bitch from New Orleans, by then a venerable great-grandmother whose snout had turned so white that she looked like a polar bear, quickly sized up the situation and settled down into a meek acceptance of her new position at the bottom of the pecking order. As it turned out, she reaped unexpected rewards by doing so—unexpected, that is, by me. Because of her meekness she made herself acceptable to the two little girls, who in no time became so fond of stroking her, pulling her grizzled head onto their laps, kissing her ears and having their noses licked, that, instead of jealousy gazing from underneath the coffee table, it now gazed gloomily from Daddy's chair. All the spontaneous physical expressions of affection that rightfully belonged to me were lavished on the sly old bitch who, with an occasional madam's glance in my direction to check if she weren't going too far this time, let herself be smooched, hugged, kissed, fed Life-Savers and Girl Scout cookies until, far from finding herself expelled from the circle of family affection, she became its center. The other dog, dim-witted as males will be, could not follow her on this winding path of feminine wiles; he went on growling, steeped in mindless envy, and finally he left. He had occasionally run away in the past, to come back the next day looking sheepish and, on one

memorable occasion when we were moored in a naval
port, smelling of cheap perfume; he had never before left
the ship or the house for more than one night at a time.
Suddenly, he vanished for weeks. We put an advertise-
ment in the local paper, we notified the police and the
humane societies of the surrounding counties, we asked
the veterinarian who had last given him a rabies shot to
be prepared for a telephone call announcing he had been
picked up miles away; in actual fact he was living right
next door to us all that time, with an elderly neighbor
who divided his time between looking at television at
night and reading the newspaper by day and who had
not realized that the dog belonged to us. Both my neighbor and myself were embarrassed at the discovery that he
was mine; he returned home with badly acted enthusiasm,
lived under our roof for one more day, which he spent
asleep underneath the kitchen counter, growling whenever one of the children came near; the next morning he
vanished again. Being dim-witted, he went back to the
neighbor next door and stayed there by mutual consent
until the neighbor went to California. It did not take him
long to find other prospects: he soon made his home a
few houses down the road where an elderly couple stayed
for the winter. The mailman, the milkman, the gas man,
all of them told us in turn that our dog had been kidnapped; I had to explain to them all that this was by mutual consent and that he would probably stay there until
his present hosts, in their turn, would leave the state. The
vet said it was senility, my wife supposed it was dim-
wittedness aged to perfection; I was convinced that he
had come to the conclusion that there was no room in the
same house for him and two little children, especially not

since the sneaky bitch had somehow managed to claim it all, and more. There was no point in reassuring him, taking him for walks, plying him with Milk-Bone, Dog-Yummies and the scraps of the children's hamburgers— he had had it. In the end, after the kind people down the road had brought him back six times only to see him turn up again the next morning, they accepted the inevitable and agreed, before they left, that he should be flown to New Bedford, Massachusetts, when they gave the word. And that is where he lives now—we hope happily ever after.

I miss him, I must confess. He was a fine ship's dog; whenever the engine was started he raced to the helmsman's seat, jumped onto it and stayed there until the end of the watch; I sailed many thousands of miles with this faithful companion at my side. I suspect that what he missed most was the sea; he did not receive the blessing of new fatherhood in his dotage to help him get over the dumb, dull yearning for the life that had been our youth.

Cats have an easier time, as they do not care too much about personal affection and lead a more independent existence. But dogs really suffer; you should, after it has become obvious that adjustment is not forthcoming, seriously consider giving him away for his own sake as well as your children's. You will be surprised how many men, especially elderly widowers, will sympathize instantly with the fate of a dog starved of affection by the arrival of a child in the household. If you are lucky enough to find such a person, this empathy may well form the basis for an autumnal revival of the ancient comradeship between man and dog.

29

Other Animals

You may discover, especially if your child is from Vietnam, that he has a more adult relationship with animals than most American children not born on a farm. Most Vietnamese children are the offspring of peasants; from early childhood they have been familiar with the animals their families raised for food. The average American child rarely associates milk with cows but with a cardboard container; of all animals other than pets he is probably most familiar with reindeer.

Some parents have found that their Vietnamese son or daughter seemed listless and lost, as if missing his family, but perked up at once when they hit upon the idea of giving him an animal to look after. If the child is fortunate enough to end up on a farm, this would be one of the first things his new parents would think of; but in an apartment in a city or a duplex in a suburb, cows, pigs, goats or even rabbits may pose a problem. It doesn't really matter how large the animal is; any animal, even a mouse will do, as long as it is made clear that it belongs to the child and no one else. This really is the secret; give him an animal that is not a family pet, and give him the sole responsibility for its care.

You may be surprised by his reaction: suddenly his sulking will stop, his somber staring out the window at an unfamiliar, hostile world will make way for delighted gazing at hamster, guinea pig or deodorized skunk, whatever your other children will be least interested in.

30

Punishment

As a Quaker I am supposed to be gentle, forbearing, understanding and averse to violence at all times. To punish children corporally is un-Quakerly; to slam poor, abandoned Asian orphans in the pants, even under the severest provocation, is a disgrace.

Even so, there are times—as when one little sister gloatingly dismembers the other little sister's favorite doll, or a five-year-old sits down on the floor with the mulish determination not to budge—when no other catharsis seems possible to the current mini-tragedy than to smack the poor mite on her abandoned little behind and carry her, accompanied by howls, shrieks and trampling fury, to whatever destination I may have in my tyrannical mind. Afterward, of course, I find myself shaken with remorse and steeped in the gloom of moral failure; but what never fails to astound me is the effect this disgraceful show of brute force has on the recipient. In no time at all she emerges, radiant, in the living room, full of charm, high spirits and the selfless desire to lay the table because Mummy is so tired. Mummy is nothing of the kind; Mummy goes quietly about her business, somehow managing to express disapproval of the incident with her back. Her disapproval does not disturb me unduly; tomorrow or the next day it will be I, quietly going about my business without demonstrating by any outward sign how utterly I disapprove of her spanking a defenseless four-year-old for no graver sin than that she has drawn a "pussing cat" on the wallpaper with a laundry marker.

Never, so some experts tell us, strike a child in anger. I admit to being an amateur, but I can't help feeling that anger is the only justification for such outbursts, at least from the child's point of view. Anger is something children readily understand, certainly our children from Asia, who have witnessed during their early lives a goodly number of adult explosions. Our children know the exact flash point of both Mummy and Daddy; in some way, utterly confounding to an apostle of nonviolence, they seem to derive comfort from an occasional reassurance that the finely honed edge of their judgment has not been blunted by too long a period of merely gentle persuasion. Maybe it is the fact that, after the act, both Mummy and Daddy are so visibly racked by remorse and so full of the most profitable contrition that to pay for all this with a mere slap on your bottom seems a bargain.

I must confess at this point that, in our case, occasions for outbursts of parental anger have gradually become rarer as time goes by. Our children are as naughty as before, but it is the kind of naughtiness everyone can live with without throwing tantrums. A year is about the time it took to reach these placid waters. One should always be careful with this kind of statement; chances are that tomorrow or the next day I will be forced to eat my words. But the fact remains that we have now lived for about six months without blow-ups, and everyone seems to be breathing easier for it. Maybe this is the road we had to travel in order to end up, however temporarily, in the peaceable kingdom of mutual trust and affection.

31

Rewards

VIOLENCE and punishment are indeed less effective than rewards. The benign, untidy gentlemen who do the dog acts in vaudeville developed those baggy pockets in their tweed jackets because they are permanently filled with goodies. After every little trick you will see them reward with a dog biscuit or a sugar lump the little mutts that walk on their hind legs, turn cartwheels and leap onto their masters' shoulders in one bound as if fired from a trap.

In the case of children, the same applies: you achieve more by rewarding their positive actions than by punishing them for their negative ones. Alas, parents are, on the whole, bad psychologists who got their children as the result of an eruption of spontaneous emotion; they bang, shriek, threaten, bellow and slam the table rather than smile benignly when their kids do wrong and give them a cookie when they do right.

To know the proper psychological approach is a comfort, however, even if you are incapable of putting it into practice. There will come a moment sooner or later when, as a result of a welcome martini or during the afterglow of some piece of shameless flattery, the mediocre parent will find himself in the mood to try doing the right thing instead of ricocheting off the walls.

The rewarding part of such an experiment in proper parental behavior is that usually it does not work. The obstreperous child, conditioned to violence following his misdeeds as thunder follows lightning, reacts to the dog-trainer's act with uneasy suspicion which expresses itself in surliness, enabling the parent to return to slam-bang fatherhood with a sense of justification.

I have to report, reluctantly, that in my case the animal-trainer and the psychologist were proven right after all. After batting a brood of four through childhood and adolescence with unbecoming raucousness and flailing of limbs, I found myself in middle age in the position of having to accept non-violence in education because I lacked the stamina for the more virile system of my younger days. They say that age brings wisdom; it also brings breathlessness, a secret past replete with mortal sins and an increasing sentimentality about young animals, from kittens to toddlers, that makes the human male in his pre-dotage particularly susceptible to the feminine wiles of four-year-old girls. In my youth I could spank a son with conviction because he had chased a neighbor's daughter with a toad, but in my dignified maturity, after some chasing of my own I can no longer mete out the same retribution with the same conviction. Sins may darken our future in eternity, but they make for an under-

standing of other people's transgressions and for help-
lessness in the face of innocence. I can no longer rise in
Mosaic anger when a child of four slams both fists on my
sacred typewriter, singing, "I wish you a Merry Christmas, I wish you a Merry Christmas, I wish you a Merry
Christmas and a Happy New Ear." Finding traces of
miniature digestion floating in the toilet no longer makes
me bellow as if hit in a buttock by an arrow, it makes me
stare with mellow melancholy, while sentimental reflec-
tions on the evanescence of man flood my aging brain. I
realize that my newfound patience with tricycles in the
driveway at dead of night or drowned dolls in the bottom of a bath filled with cold soapy water is caused by
age rather than conversion; even so, it enabled me to discover that to reward a child for acts of kindness and generosity rather than berating him for the opposite is more
effective in the long run. It also makes for an atmosphere
in the house that will eventually get the better of even
the most proficient whiner.

Especially in the case of our children, the boost of
praise and the balm of admiration will help heal old
wounds and soothe sorrows that never reach the surface.
Why punish the bird that trails a broken wing for turning on us, hissing defiantly? There they are, all alone in
an unknown world, haunted by the irrevocable farewell
to all they knew and loved; how can we lift a hand in
anger and strike them for bouncing on the furniture or
dropping their sister's hair-band down the elevator shaft?
Yet our own imperfections and the sins of our fathers
compel us to treat them as if all they had ever known was
the security of our home, the shelter of our love, the
comfort of our affluence.

After one occasion, when the old Adam in me had won out over the meekness of the New Testament in my reaction to one daughter's transgression and I had given her a spanking that left me abjectly guilty, I called up the adoptive father of three Korean kids who were model children. He listened to my confession and said, "I know it will sound simplistic to you, but I assure you that no psychologist, however understanding, and no animal-trainer with pockets full of goodies can give your child what you gave her today."

"What is that?" I asked, somberly.

"The knowledge that you care," he replied. "The psychologist treats children because that happens to be the way he makes his living; the trainer doesn't train his little dog to help it realize its potentials, but because it happens to be the way *he* makes his living. Your child knows that you like her for her own sake, and at times detest her for her own sake, but that at all times she is your daughter. She may have become your daughter because you painted yourself into a corner, you may have acted out of selfishness rather than compassion, it doesn't matter. There she is, and there you are, and you are stuck together as father and daughter whether you make the best of it or the worst. This simple fact, that you have somehow become father and daughter, makes all the difference in the world; you are allowed to do with impunity what no other man could do, because between father and daughter anger happens to be a proof of concern."

It was a good speech and it sounded convincing; I envied him his wisdom and his mature detachment. But I went on carrying the cross of remorse, be it made of balsa wood, convinced that in this case my anger had brought about an irreparable estrangement. The next morning I took her to school in the car; as we drove along the freeway at high speed in silence, she suddenly asked, "Daddy, will you be beside me when I die?"

I looked at her with astonishment that turned into incredulous relief when I saw the innocent sincerity on her solemn little face.

"I—I certainly hope so," I replied, foolishly, "I'll—I'll certainly do my best."

It was, considered with the detachment of the professional, probably the wrong answer, but the car that had until then raced down the highway with ill-tempered speed slowed down, so as not to make her question timely, and trundled on to school virtually wagging its tail.

32

Awareness

ONE of the things that will amaze you, especially if your child is over four years old, is his uncanny awareness of your moods, which at times will make him seem to be far ahead of his age. One mother said to me recently, "Yes, we are doing fine. She is a delightful little girl. Only, you know, at times she can look at me as if the whole child bit was make-believe and in reality she was thirty years old."

The answer is that she is both. All Asian children who come to us for adoption, especially those who are no longer infants, have survived only because they have developed an uncanny awareness of the shifting moods of the adults around them. The stereotyped concept of the imperturbable Oriental does not apply to the social stratum in which these children lived. Violence, brutality and lust were not confined, as in the case of most American children, to television; in Asia they were realities and, rather than learning how to live with them, our children were forced to learn how to survive them. They had to develop an aptitude for foreseeing any adult outburst so they could scurry in time; those who failed to scurry did not live to tell the tale.

One thing you can be sure of: whatever happens between the two of you, when it becomes really necessary your Asian child will know how to handle almost any situation. He will know the weather signs that indicate an imminent change in your mood better than you know them yourself; when the mood changes he will either know how to handle you or be gone. No wonder this disturbed the mother whose five-year-old child seemed at times to be thirty. We may think, in moments of self-commiseration, that all we want is to be understood; to find we are being understood by a child of five is an unnerving experience.

In time, the perspicacity of our children is something one comes to appreciate rather than deplore. Marjorie and I discovered that this uncanny awareness of our moods and thoughts gradually took on a more positive aspect, expressing itself in an occasional unchildlike concern for our welfare. It was pretty disconcerting, the first time, to hear my elder daughter, aged six, say one evening before supper, "Daddy, you look tired. Sit down here and read the paper. I'll get your glasses for you."

As I obeyed, baffled and delighted, I felt all the same that slight uneasiness again. Was it natural, I asked myself, for a child of her age to be so solicitous? Memories from my own childhood prompted me to conclude that she must be after something, and this made my reaction to her concern somewhat less spontaneous than it might have been. But my suspicion was unfounded. What I was witnessing was the same awareness of adults' moods, thoughts and hidden intentions that had once disturbed me so. Like most talents, it can be used either destructively or creatively; once your child has lived for a while in an atmosphere of kindness and consideration for others, you will find, in your turn, that his awareness of your moods gradually changes into concern.

It is one of those unexpected things that seem like a Divine affirmation, a sign that all is well. It is worth waiting for, and it may be a help to know about it when, in the early stages of your life together, you find your child watching you with eyes that are thirty years old.

33

Nightmares

MANY parents report that after the first month a new trial is added: nightmares. For several weeks the child will wake up in the middle of the night, screaming, to tell you incoherently about a bad dream, seeing bad people or guns. When you pick him up and comfort him you may reminisce with nostalgia on those early days when, after the first few trying nights when everything was still strange and new, he went to bed so calmly and slept through the night without a sound. But rather than mourn those nights of peace and quiet you should rejoice that your child has finally begun to feel a tentative sense of security. For, oddly enough, that is what the nightmare indicates. In the beginning he simply had to sleep in order to recover from the great transition; now that he begins to unwind, his subsconscious fears and worries are given a chance to manifest themselves without the heavy lid of total emotional exhaustion weighting down the manhole through which, at dead of night, the ghosts come crawling.

Of course it is superficial to generalize; each child will present a personal pattern. But of two things you can be sure: the nightmares will start only after he has been with you for some time; and, rather than taking them as a sign that your troubles are about to start, you should welcome them as a reassurance that your real trouble is over. Contrary to what you might expect, your child is not yearning wholeheartedly for security. The past has taught him to mistrust all adult protection. He comes to you convinced, in his own inarticulate but by no means subconscious way, that the only true security can be found in standing on his own feet. He will, without showing it, be fighting against the temptation I mentioned before: your affection, luring him back into the simple trustfulness of childhood. But now that the demands of his tender years are winning out over his precocious maturity he will be unable to resist the siren call of your tenderness. The distraught dreamer waking up at dead of night with screams of terror and anguish is the lone wolf, who once found a stunted sense of security in the very fact of his isolation, being drawn back inexorably into the child he was never allowed to be.

What you need most at this point is patience, as you would with an infant who has to be fed during the night. He needs the same: your infinite, seraphic patience, which at his less appealing age, alas, is much harder to come by.

34

Whining

I SUPPOSE every parent has his pet aversion, one aspect of
his children's behavior that despite all good intentions
and accumulated wisdom sets him off like a rocket. Mine
happens to be whining.

I suppose it all goes back to my early childhood. We
were a happy family, gay and affectionate; one of us,
however, was prone to sudden "moods." For no apparent reason, triggered by the most inconsequential incident,
he would freeze, his face set into a scowl, and he would
sit at the breakfast table or in a jolly gathering of friends
poisoning the atmosphere as surely as if he had set off a
stink bomb. In later life, on board ship, I occasionally
came across people suffering from this affliction; although I was a pleasant—be it undistinguished—skipper,
this was one thing that turned me into Captain Bligh: I
would order the offender to leave the messroom as if he
were a child. I have always felt that to terrorize a family

or a ship's crew with "moods" was intolerable; I suppose it is another proof of God's sense of humor that, in the autumn of my life, I am blessed with two little daughters who have perfected the judicious application of moods to a fine art.

It started virtually the day they arrived. If anything did not quite go their way, if they were refused a fifteenth cookie or thwarted in their inalienable right to improve on the design of the wallpaper of our rented house by finger-painting, they would sit down on floor, chair or bed, freeze to motionlessness and start spreading concentric rings of gloom with the penetrating force of a radio beacon.

Because of their diminutive size, I was able to do what I had not been able to do to third mate or wireless operator, which was to take them under my arm, put them in their room and slam the door. My absolute refusal to suffer one single minute of terrorism by mood made them snap out of it fairly rapidly; like most of their uncontrollable emotions, this one tended to wither the moment the actor was separated from his audience. But they found something to replace it with that proved even more effective; in a sense it was the same thing, wired for sound. They started to whine.

If something did not go their way, if et cetera, et cetera, they would pull their faces into a scowl and start to emit a plaintive, woeful sound that, if countered by parental anger or irritation, would gleefully increase to a keening lamentation and ultimately crest triumphantly in boo-hoos, blubberings and buckets of tears. With the unerring perspicacity of children, especially these children, they spotted with a radar eye that Daddy's reaction to their whining was self-defeating; if they could keep it up until he exploded into Dutch expletives, he would afterward be so crestfallen that the whole operation might well end as a profitable one for the inhabitants of Lilliput.

So, if ever you should be warned that my advice is biased, it is on the subject of whining. I must confess that I have not the faintest idea how to cope with it effectively; all I know is that, if you are like me and a few other people I know, it will drive you around the bend in three seconds flat. You will threaten, you will order, you will yell, and from there to going down on your knees in abject apology is but a bum's rush down the steep slope of shame. There you are: six feet tall, two hundred pounds after a day's fasting and a laxative, and there she is: three feet nothing, weighing less than a medium-sized dog, and you bawled her out as if . . . But, seriously: what *does* one do in the face of this infuriating blackmail, which is what whining really amounts to? Older and wiser fathers tell me that the child will grow out of it; my wife suggests that, rather than respond with the apoplectic roar of a Saturn rocket at blast-off, I should absent myself with a wistful smile and go and dig a hole in the garden, hurling sods onto the roof while she calmly deals with the little beasts in private. I am sure that this would be the most sensible, reasonable and educationally sound reaction; but I am forced to confess that some deep satisfaction, some subliminal relish in my own coming apart at the seams, tends to prevent me from going out into the garden to dig a hole before I have impersonated a motorcyclist after a wasp has flown into his sleeve.

Contrite as I may be afterward and aware as I may be of the exorbitant exaggeration of my reaction, somewhere in the back of my mind I have always had the ultimate excuse that in one respect at least I was a better person than the mini-monster that had needled me into this elephantine rage: I was a man without moods who had never whined. Then my brother came to stay for a week, which gave him a chance to become intimately acquainted with his new little nieces and be corrupted from a skeptical doubter into a drooling adulator. He was also given a chance to be present at one of the little corridas in which Daddy figured as the bull, his four-year-old daughter as the matador, while her six-year-old sister deftly implanted the banderillas. The trumpet that preceded the entry of El Toro had been the whining the youngest one resorted to when not allowed to slice her toast herself with a steak knife honed for surgery. When it was all over and the two old men, bemused and thoughtful, were sitting in their rocking chairs overlooking the sea, my brother said, "You know, when you told me in one of your letters that the little one mysteriously began to show character traits that were clearly yours, I didn't believe it. But now I must admit you have something. It's extraordinary."

"What makes you say that?" I inquired, feigning interest, but still steeped in the gloom of the aftermath, which was not surprising considering that to all intents and purposes my bull's ears had been distributed among the audience and that I had cut off my tail myself.

"Don't you remember?" my brother asked, surprised. "You used to whine exactly like that; you drove everybody crazy with it."

"You're kidding . . . ," I said, with a sinking feeling in my stomach. This could not be true, it simply couldn't. I had many faults, but whining . . .

"Yes," he continued, his reminiscing now tinged with a hint of malice that transported me back fifty years. "It was the one sure thing to set Dad snorting like a bull. Next thing we knew, the breakfast table had turned into a three-ring circus. You really did have it down to a fine art."

I sat for a moment in silence. Then I said, "Oh."

I report this incident because, whatever your pet aversion may be in the arsenal of your children's weapons, it would be wise to consult someone who knew you when you were little before you enter the ring. It will not stop you from blowing up, but it will stop you from blowing up in righteousness. And that, so my brother and I agreed, is the surest way to make your children loathe you.

35

Values

WHEN your child arrives from Asia, he has to exchange one complete set of values for another; you cannot expect him to be able to discern between frugality and luxury according to our standards until later. The new world is so strange, so utterly different in all respects, that the thought will never occur to him that a car is a necessity of life but a motorboat a luxury, nor will he see any difference in value between a black-and-white television set and a color set.

There will be occasions when the values of the community he left behind become apparent. If, for instance, you are in the habit of having a drink before dinner with which you serve salted peanuts, he will eye the little dish with intense anticipation. After you have settled down he will sidle up to you, point at the peanuts with his cutest smile and ask, "May I?" When you say, "Sure, go ahead," he will ask, "One?"

147

Were you to allow him just one peanut, he would not consider you stingy or, as children from our affluent culture might, off your rocker; he would judge this a reasonable gift and turn away content.

Of course this paradisical state of affairs is not going to last. Soon, especially after he has started school, the old values of frugality he brought with him will be replaced by whatever the values and the standards are among the kids of your community. But behind those there will always be, as long as he lives, some memories of the old standard of living, by which anything not strictly necessary for mere survival was considered a windfall to be grabbed with gratitude and lightning speed before anyone else did. It is the key to some mysterious reactions that may seem to be out of all proportion. It is the key to the little girl sobbing her heart out in a room full of expensive dolls, toy kitchens, boxes of crayons and a stack of coloring books because she had lost a plastic spoon that came, free, with a dish of ice cream three weeks earlier. It was the key to the mysterious behavior of my elder daughter on one occasion. She had been with us for many months; that day, tired of her pestering me with cat's cradles, I took the length of yarn away from her and stuffed it in my mouth, pretending to eat it. To my surprise and alarm, she burst into uncontrollable sobs; only when the yarn was given back to her, after having been dried surreptitiously on the seat of my contrite pants, did she relent. She never could discover anything funny in my lame but well-intentioned joke; judged by the standards of her past, I had revealed myself as an ogre, living on a diet of toys, yanked away from playing children.

36

"*Testing, Testing . . .*"

EVERY child is naughty at times, every child gives its parents insomnia, nervous indigestion and periods of bewilderment during which they will sit on the sofa, hand in hand and close together, in stunned incredulity that someone so small, whom they love so much, could have done such a malicious, outrageous, utterly incomprehensible thing, such as sitting on the head of a younger brother until he passed out, or setting fire to a stack of newspapers underneath the house with the obvious intention of burning it down, or covering the floor of the entrance porch with shaving foam so that Aunt Paula, skidding like an airplane making a belly landing, crashed on her mercifully huge behind. The question that sums up these situations is "Why?" Why should a perfectly normal, happy, well-fed, comfortably housed and tenderly loved child want to *do* these things?

Now here is one area, at last, where the adoptive parents of Asian children have a distinct advantage: they can answer the question "Why?" with the words, "Never mind, dear, he is testing again."

Indeed, some of our children's aberrations can be explained by their recurrent desire to reassure themselves that we will go on liking them despite their behavior. But not all their monkeyshines should be exonerated by this lofty interpretation. Should we find our darling underneath a wooden porch in the process of setting fire to one of its supports, he is not testing the strength of his parents' affection, he is testing what will happen if one sets fire to one of the supports of a wooden porch. I have done it myself.

Our children are full of pranks that are symptoms not of insecurity but of sheer high spirits. They are buzzing with vitality, have more energy than they know what to do with, are on the whole extremely intelligent; all of this will express itself, alas, in inventive mischief and not in reciting the Gettysburg Address by our bedside. Our two little daughters were given a swing-and-slide set in the garden for Christmas, guaranteed by the makers to be harmless whatever the kiddies might dream up; within the hour the two of them had devised five different methods by which the manufacturer could be sued for involuntary manslaughter.

The best way of dealing with our children's testing is to respond, without reticence, with the reaction that comes naturally to us. To withhold a reprimand or to sublimate our exasperation out of respect for their inner insecurity will only tend to give our reaction to subsequent tests a higher number of megatons. Marjorie and I found it benefited all concerned to tell our children, when they started cutting up at table, to pipe down or be banished to the kitchen where they could finish their meal alone. When we were still putting up with it on the consideration that they were testing, we discovered that we would blast the pants off them later that night, when they drenched the bathroom floor by coordinated sloshing. We concluded that if our children were testing we should give them some reliable results, and that what they were really testing was not the depth of our love but the limits of our endurance.

Some people get mad at whiners, others at noise, others again at tattletales; the child has a right to know in which class you belong, so that once this has been established he can go about the business of daily living with a reliable set of ground rules. The security he wants most, at least for the time being, is to know exactly how far he can go before blast-off; the sooner you oblige him with this information, the sooner you will treat him the way he wants to be treated: like any normal child.

37

Sense of Humor

SOME nations have a sense of humor more congenial to us than others. British wit is very different from German humor; the Dutch wouldn't begin to understand a Russian joke. I would be inclined to say, personally, that Korean humor is more akin to my own than Vietnamese. The latter is subtle, while Korean humor has a streak of bawdiness and anger rather reminiscent of the Dutch.

There is, for example, the story of a Korean brothel, ordered by the current American general to either desist corrupting his young men or close. It obediently put a sign on its door saying, "No more whorehouse, trying to be laundry; welcome General X." The word "trying" is the key.

What saves the Koreans, dour as they may be at times, from boorishness is this streak of droll defiance. There comes a moment when, driven beyond the bounds of behavior considered proper by Confucius, they will explode in maddened anger, expressing itself in a surrealist bawdiness that at times becomes sheer poetry. The Vietnamese, after a millennium of Chinese influence and a century of French occupation, turn subtle and precise as their anger mounts, until they find solace for their outraged sense of dignity by exchanging, smiling seraphically, little flitting jokes between themselves over the head of the foreigner who finds himself in between.

You will discover as time goes by that your child in some measure represents one of these divergent characteristics. Most Korean children will, in moments of rebellion or exasperation, show a sudden fury that may at times give you the uncomfortable feeling that, so far, you have only scratched the surface of their true nature. This, let me reassure you, is not so; you have not been the victim of diabolical duplicity when you think of your Korean child as spontaneous, ingenuous and engagingly frank. But there is that sudden, blazing fury, that maddened explosiveness, which will at times open up like a safety valve and shriek fit to raise the roof. Confronted with this phenomenon, the best solution is to leave the banshee to his own devices; as I said before, the only thing that will deflate these born hams is the loss of their audience.

The blessed usefulness of a sense of humor is that it presents the Achilles' heel of its possessor. In almost any situation of uncontrollable grief, righteous indignation or all-consuming anger, the Asian child with a sense of humor will collapse in angry giggles the moment you make him aware of the ridiculousness of the situation. This can never be done by direct reference to his performance; it would involve a loss of face to laugh at himself. But underneath the sound and the fury there is a sense of proportion, a readiness to escape into laughter that may make even the lamest joke a powerful distraction.

I cannot speak from experience, but it seems that Vietnamese children, whose sense of humor is in no way inferior to that of the Korean children although rather more refined, are not as easily diverted as their more temperamental northern cousins. The Vietnamese child will more readily consider his dignity impaired; while humor is the perfect debunker of any theatrical display of emotion, it will tend to aggravate any insult, real or imaginary, to the dignity of the individual. Given their delicate and graceful physical characteristics, this may well be the only defense the frail Vietnamese have against the boisterous bawdiness shared by Dutchman, Yankee, Irishman and Korean alike, though it does not necessarily unite them.

The ones who seem to me to combine the best of both worlds are Korean girls. Maybe because they are considered inferior by the men, they have developed over the centuries a demure mischievousness, an elusive twinkle of quicksilvery mirth that I, for one, find utterly irresistible. But, considering the make-up of my family, I may be prejudiced.

38

Lying

Iт depends on where you draw the line. In countries with
a puritan history like Holland, anything that does not
state the facts as soberly as a traffic ticket is called a lie.
Although my parents were a little more lenient and con-
sequently suspect in the eyes of the staider members of
our community, I had a number of elderly maiden aunts
who were not prepared to sell out for a pleading look, a
beguiling smile or whatever else a six-year-old liar had up
his sleeve. Two of them, sisters who shared a small low
house overlooking the harbor which was often photographed by tourists because they thought they had seen
it in a painting by Vermeer, were the sternest of my
judges. Such is the power of hereditary values that until
this day their stern faces stare at me accusingly across the
widening gulf of time. Most people are admonished by a
small, still voice; I am by a small, still duet.

After I had written my first book I took it to them,

together with, as a precaution, a large box of chocolate cherries. They accepted the cherries, not the book. One of them leafed through it, asked, "Did all this really happen?" When I hedged in my answer, trying to explain the principle of art which Renoir once formulated as "man's obligation to correct nature," she closed the book with a gesture that indicated she was not going to open it again and said calmly, "I am grateful that Aunt Clara and I are about to leave this vale of tears; I don't think we are at home here any longer." When, obediently, I picked up my cue and asked, "Why, Aunt Minna?" she answered, with a look that still haunts my adult dreams, "Until now you were punished for your lies; in future I gather you will be paid for them."

Other people, of whom I shamefacedly confess to be one, consider untruths to be lies only when they are inspired by laziness, fear of punishment or the desire to transfer one's guilt to another person; in our house this usually is the liar's sister, although the dogs have at times been accused by our children of climbing onto the kitchen counter to raid the cookie jar or defoliate a budding avocado on the window sill. As a consequence of this attitude we have an easier time with our daughters than Aunties Clara and Minna would have had with these little heathen from Asia, but I admit that we may be losing in virtue what we gain in comfort.

When a three-year-old, in tiny dressing gown and furry slippers with bunnies on them, her hair freshly plastered after the bath, comes into the living room and finds it peopled with giants holding glasses, shouting opinions at one another, I can identify with the impulse that makes her state, looking up at the swaying torsos above the trousers and the mini-skirts, "I saw a moo-cow." When nobody pays any attention, because nobody has noticed the gnome in bunny slippers who has infiltrated their ranks, I am stricken with admiration when I hear her say, louder, "I saw a moo-cow on a motorbike!" Despite their merely peripheral awareness of the little voice, our guests cannot escape the image of a cow sitting upright on a narrow saddle, front hoofs on the handlebars; it makes the monologues falter because of such involuntary thoughts as "How uncomfortable that must be, with one's udder on the gas tank." To me, this represents the first miraculous stirring of the power of evocation which is the secret of all art; the Aunties Minna and Clara would have gasped at this manifestation of man's original sin.

Children talk about everything, especially the past, as if they heartily approved of Renoir's precept. They do not embellish the truth, they merely report what they saw and experienced at a time when their concept of reality must have corresponded with that of a wise old baboon. Our children show the same tendency; where they differ from other children is that to them the past has a traumatic quality. It is hard for us, who have led fairly sheltered lives particularly during our early childhood, to gauge the emotional trauma suffered as a result of the slow, agonizing death of one identity concurrent with the slow, agonizing birth of another. The dividing line between the little peasant boy in Vietnam and young John Jones in America is as final as the one between our earthly existence and life hereafter. In his previous incarnation as Nguyen van Thuan, John Jones had a mother who carried huge loads on her head and beat the laundry on flat stones at the water's edge, and a father who smelled of fish, had hard, callused hands and occasionally took him out in his sampan. These people were as real to him as you are now; they had a different smell, spoke a different language, treated him differently; his childhood, seen from the great beyond, has absolutely nothing in common with the reality in which he now exists. He is no longer himself but somebody totally new, a different child with a different name and, probably, a different character. Somehow, John Jones has to come to terms with Nguyen van Thuan and relate him to this new child wearing blue jeans and sneakers, riding a bicycle and eating more food for breakfast than the other always hungry one could hope to see in a day. It is a miracle that so very few of our children show any permanent damage as a result of this experience, which would throw most adults on our side of the Pacific sobbing onto the couch of a psychiatrist. Even the Aunties Minna and Clara among us will have to modify their incorruptible standards of what constitutes truth and what falsehood, at least until the child has had a chance to find his feet in the new reality.

The past will not be discussed at all during the first weeks, and only very tentatively thereafter. As time goes by, the image of that past as recalled by the child will undergo fundamental changes. Whereas, at first, the skeletal fisherman with his loincloth and coolie hat and the mother in her black pajamas will be poor and hungry, gradually these two basic characters in what will rapidly become a fairytale will be affluent, well dressed, surrounded by Western comforts, rather like his present parents only they will be more permissive and attentive. Little Hwa Ran Park, at first depicted as a scruffy urchin, always itching, dressed only in an undershirt, running barefoot around the straw hut that was her home while playing tag with neighboring children, will change into a little princess, pretty and pampered, surrounded by dogs and pussy-cats, riding side-saddle on a water buffalo's back, her gown of silk fluttering in the wind or lazily swinging with the animal's gait. The airplane which took her from one life to the other, at first described in realistic detail complete with who threw up and which child wet his pants, will turn into an airplane unlike all others, a living being of gigantic proportions, like the legendary goose that wings its way through the sagas of the Scandinavian nations.

What you are witnessing is not, as you might assume, the new child giving the old a sumptuous burial in the soil of her subconscious; it is the new child absorbing the old as an integral part of herself, which at her age can only be done in terms that symbolize the past rather than chronicle it.

Whatever way the past is interpreted, it should never be treated as a lie and the child should never be confronted with inconsistencies. For, in a sense more real than any of us can imagine, our children during their first year under our roof are in the process of being reborn.

39

Stealing

You may never come up against this; if you do, you should understand that you are not burdened with a dishonest, delinquent child but entrusted with a disturbed one. The cause for his disturbance is recent, he has not necessarily been damaged emotionally in any permanent sense. But it may depend to a large extent on what you do now, when you first discover this propensity, whether the shock his young and fragile personality has suffered will pass off harmlessly.

To start with, you should realize that life in an orphanage, certainly in Vietnam and often in Korea, is the reverse of what it might be assumed to be by those who know only the orphanages in our own country. An orphan's life in an institution in Asia is an unending struggle for survival; anything he can lay his hands on, be it food, clothing, or the small seeds of solitary fantasies like a coin, a little shell or a button off a uniform, has to be guarded with tooth and claw against marauders among his fellow inmates, especially the older ones. One couple, who received their newly adopted little son from Korea just before Christmas, were deeply distressed when the child made off with his presents to his room without opening them and hid them under his bed. The mother, after waiting for over a week, finally ran out of patience, dragged the packages from under the bed despite his desperate protests and unwrapped them herself. It was an understandable act of exasperation, but not a very sensible one. The child had merely reacted with a conditioned reflex which in this new and bewildering world suddenly no longer made sense.

The fact is that this transition from one world to another is as traumatic as birth. What the child will need for a long time is your reassurance that, whoever he may turn out to be, you are delighted to have him with you and positively relieved that he is turning out the way he is. You may find this difficult when you are faced with his stealing not just food or a toy, but something of value. You have given him all he could wish for, he knows that he only has to point and he shall be given to a degree where you have wondered if you aren't going too far; now why does this crazy child have to make off with your pocketbook and hide it under his pillow?

The first thing to recognize is that he has not hidden it. If he really wanted to hide it, he would not have put it underneath his pillow, unless he makes his own bed. Probably you do that for him; during those first days there is simply not enough for you to do to satisfy your compulsion to show him how welcome he is, how ready you are to love him, how you hope and pray that he will relax and be himself and trust you and take it easy. Well, that's exactly what he has tentatively started to do. This child, expelled from home and country and sent all alone across a terrifying void to land dazed with shock and sick with exhaustion in Siloville, Nebraska, is your friend, however incomprehensible and mysterious his motivations may seem to you. Be sensible, where could he have gone with your pocketbook? What good would it have done him? He doesn't understand any of its contents, he has no notion of the purpose or value of objects such as lipstick, compact wallet with credit cards, or the dainty box with a month's supply of the pill. The only object that might have meant something to him would have been a rabbit's foot, if you carried one for luck, although his conclusion would probably have been that it was the remnant of a snack. His stealing it was a symbolic act, made up of two components: one, the desire to find out whether you really meant it when you gave him to understand that you liked him; the other, a playful gesture of challenge that he himself is not sure of but tries anyhow because something in him, craving for expression, compels him to do it.

How should you react? You should understand what he himself has not quite understood—namely, that it's a game. You should join in by finding the pocketbook after a long and dramatic search, making it obvious when you find it that the whole thing has been exaggerated play-acting on your part; then you say, "So *that's* where it is!" and hug him. Although you suspect that he will recoil from it, you might even kiss him lightly; this could well be the first time he will let you do so. For what you have done is to confirm the rightness of his instinctive impulse. He is on the right track; he may not yet understand what this new world is all about, but at least it is a world with which he has, he now finds, some basic affinity.

So, although it may be rough going, try to put into practice the tired platitude that it always pays off to assume the best about people. For you are dealing with a disoriented, scared and desperately lonely child who is trying to find out if this strange, large and rather forbidding woman with the yellow hair, the scarlet mouth and the mysterious scent of invisible flowers really wants to be, ever really can be, the one he will call his mother.

40

Running Away

AMONG the several hundred cases of interracial adoption with which I became acquainted through my correspondence with other parents, there was only one in which a child, within the first month of her arrival from Korea, ran away from home.

She was a four-year-old girl; it was her good fortune to find herself in the care of mature, experienced and level-headed parents. They lived on a dead-end street in a suburb of a big city, off a major thoroughfare busy with traffic traveling at high speed. There were other children in the family; like them, the newcomer had been told never, under any circumstances, to try to cross that highway by herself.

The first time the child announced that she was "going home" the parents, with outward calm and composure but inwardly scared stiff, managed to make it sound credible when they said, "Sure, honey, go right ahead." The child, with a display of calm and composure matching their own, casually strolled out the door. One of the other children was dispatched to see where she went, with instructions not to show himself if he could help it; he reported that she went right up to the highway, stood there on the curbside for a while watching the traffic, then turned around and calmly went back to the house. She was welcomed kindly but casually, as if the whole episode were accepted as normal by everyone concerned. The mother confessed that later that evening, in the privacy of the marital bedroom, she burst into tears. She and her husband talked it over for many hours; they concluded that, even if they had not done the right thing, this was the only way they could handle it.

A few weeks later, when the child found herself thwarted in something she wanted to do that was unacceptable, she again announced she was going home. For a second time she got up and walked out the door. This time she only went to the gate, where she dallied for a while, out of sight of her new parents; when it became obvious that she was not being followed and that no one was going to drag her back forcibly, she returned with the same show of casual indifference as before.

The third time she got no farther than the hall. She stood for a while in the doorway, looking at the garden and the gate, then she turned around and came back to the table. It was the last time she considered running away.

I don't know what Marjorie and I would have done under similar circumstances; obviously, we should react the way we feel. I just thought that it might be useful to include this story; some couple may find comfort in the knowledge that children have been known to run away before.

41

Music

MOST children from the Far East are very musical and will arrive with a collection of songs that cannot fail to charm you, once the initial unfamiliarity of the melody has worn off. Especially in the case of Korean children you may discover that their repertoire is extensive and varied; there is reason for caution, however, on two counts.

For one thing, the community from which most of these children come cherishes a number of songs concerning the basic aspects of life, with lyrics that are considerably more forthright than the naughty ditties remembered from our own schooldays. A New England university professor and his wife adopted a little Korean boy who soon after his arrival turned out to be a veritable songbird. Moved by the child's spontaneous caroling, the professor and his wife took pains to jot down phonetically the lyrics of his songs. They worked out an accompaniment on the guitar and proceeded to give spontaneous concerts on their front porch during the warm summer evenings. Only when a Korean colleague visited the campus did the professor become aware of the meaning of the words they had sung so lustily in triple descant, to the sentimental delight of their neighbors. Every single one of the songs in their repertoire furnished a play-by-play description of some elemental bodily function; the one they preferred because of its nostalgic, lilting melody and richly voweled words, so suitable for largo sostenuto, was revealed as a condensation of one of the more athletic chapters of the *Kama Sutra*. So, before you join your new child in song, make sure that you know what you are singing about.

The second cause for wariness is that most of our children not only have a productive imagination but are bent on pleasing us and putting themselves in the most congenial light. Our elder daughter, when she discovered that she could enrapture us by sitting at the organ and, idly fingering the keys in muted cacophony, accompanying herself while singing the melodious ditties of her homeland, gradually extended her repertoire until finally, alerted by words like "school bus" and "pussy-cat," we realized that she was making up her Korean songs as she went along. The moment she sensed that we were aware of this, she ruefully confined herself to the basic five, of which "Santoki," "Songadji" and "Appuflower" were the most prominent.

Our younger daughter, on the contrary, was not hampered by these inhibitions. She went on singing in her stilted English anything that came to mind, until it became a tradition for her to sit on the windowsill or on the

edge of the table after dinner to review, in song, the highlights of the day. She sang songs on "Mikey ran away"
after our old male dog had absented himself in disgust;
she signaled the arrival of the first migrating birds in our
garden and the fact that the milkman had dropped a carton of fortified homogenized on the sidewalk with a
splash pattern ideal for hopscotch. Her most haunting
and surrealist improvisation ran, "Beautiful birds, with
nothing on underneath, sit in puppy trees waiting for ice-
cream flowers."

Just as stammerers magically shed their affliction the
moment they start singing instead of speaking, children
from Asia, responding to the touch of some good fairy's
wand, seem to be able to express in song what they cannot bring themselves to say in direct confrontation. We
were first informed of our younger daughter's tentative
affection during one of her after-dinner recitals, when
she sang in the course of a dreamy, melodious improvisation, "I love my Mummy," followed instantly by, "I love
cake." As we had had a rather strenuous time with her, I
suspect that Marjorie, although I never asked her in so
many words, would gladly have exchanged Beethoven's
quartets for this single tremulous phrase, sung by a child
of three sitting on the edge of the dinner table, one unforgettable evening in spring.

42

Dancing

IF your child is a girl from Korea between three and six, she will almost certainly love to dance for you. Our daughters did; at first we thought that this passion for the ballet was exclusive to them, but communication with other parents revealed that most little girls from Korea share this passion. At the sound of any music, be it a commercial jingle or Bruckner's Fifth, they will go through a complete performance involving pirouettes, bows and graceful kicks, which at any moment may suddenly change into a bump-and-grind exhibition of a startling nature.

It must be that most of these children witnessed at a tender age, through the cracks of barroom doors, the gyrations of the dancing girls who since time immemorial have followed the train of any conquering army. If, however, you encourage the more classical stances and smile noncommittally at the other, they will concentrate on the more acceptable part of their repertoire; once they have had a chance to join a ballet class in kindergarten or first grade, those other remnants of their small past will be safely laid to rest, perchance to dream.

Somehow, you will have to come to terms with your children's past. Their dancing is only one expression of it; the songs are another. The thing to remember is that in their case sin and guilt are in the eyes of the beholder. The coarse and depressing prancings they have seen are sublimated and purified by their own innocence and by their overpowering desire to please you. What is more, to dance like that gives them a chance to integrate their past with the present; anything they can do to transplant some of the roots of their identity into our foreign soil should be encouraged. The break with the past is brutal and absolute; their tenuous lifeline was severed by a sword the night they crossed the ocean; to react with disapproval to any aspect of their repertoire is to cut back the living shoot of a plant that is trying to survive a hazardous transition.

Our children arrive in our homes in a state of total innocence; give them a chance to live in paradise for just a little while longer before the fate of man compels them to heed the snake, eat the apple and come to grief. For the time being, let them wink, jut their buttocks and grind their pelvis, as they dance around the tree of knowledge flushed with the tender green of spring.

43

Money

OUR children, especially those aged five and up, have a keen concept of the value of money. In Vietnam, whenever dusty bands of soldiers came tramping through their village, they ran out to meet them the moment it became clear that the men had either not yet fallen victim to the bright-eyed lunacy of the man-hunt or were recovering from it. Whether the roaming platoons of warriors came trudging into the hamlet beset by doubts and unspeakable memories, or marched through filled with apprehension and superstitious hope, they were in the mood to be generous to children. The same reflex that makes soldiers build orphanages with their own hands to house the children whose fathers they killed compels them to shower candy, money and cigarettes on the rapacious packs of corrupted urchins who emerge as soon as their shrewd awareness has assured them that it is safe to do so. As to the sad little denizens of the "recreation villages" along

the demarcation line between North and South Korea,
they too are familiar with soldiers, flushed with anticipation or troubled by guilt, who are in a generous mood.

We have to re-educate them so they will no longer
regard money as something to be wheedled or swindled
out of adults. The notion that money symbolizes reward
is, you will find, new to them; it is best to forget all about
it until they are settled down and the values of their new
society have had a chance to take root. They will learn
fast; just as you will be amazed at how quickly they pick
up our language, you will be surprised by the rapidity
and apparently effortless ease with which they assimilate
the outward trappings of our civilization. Soon they will
be ready for the Christian tradition of pocket money and
for the material rewards, however symbolic, for washing
the car, making the beds or raking the lawn. The longer
you postpone bestowing this blessing upon them, however, the better. Let them discover for themselves that
kindness and helpfulness, which they have so far squan-
dered upon us for nothing, in our society carry a fee.
You may be forced to knuckle under in the end to the
demands of conformity in this respect, yet you will
probably find that, even after the mercenary standards of
our culture have taken hold, some impulse will at times
prompt the children to part with all their possessions in a
sudden burst of largess. It is almost as if they felt compelled, at odd intervals that regrettably become longer as
time goes by, to deposit the symbol of their good fortune
on the altar of an unknown God. Unlike Her Britannic
Majesty, who each year at Christmastime sends an Admi-
ral and a General to deposit a gift of gold at the feet of
the newly born Son of God only to take it back to the

Bank of England after the ceremony, our children, after handing out their gift, will never look back or mention it again. They may give it to "the poor children," to clothe the naked or feed the hungry; they may even turn their money into toys and candy if the poor children are real enough.

Try to encourage this impulse without appearing to promote it. Agree with your child that it is an excellent idea when he suggests it, but if he changes the subject do not return to it of your own accord. Leave it to him to find the delicate balance between his inarticulate sense of good fortune and his equally inarticulate greed. It is one of those rituals man invents for himself and yet not entirely by himself, as if he were drawn by some distant goal, like the carrier pigeon. Every religion that is not merely a philosophy or a glorified tribal dance has for its luminous center this impulse of kindness and generosity. Without it, as we witness today, even the most prosperous and powerful society becomes a spiritual hell where all selfless impulses are either cynically exploited or equally cynically debunked. For this process of damnation there is no cure other than the power that prompts your child, after an agony of indecision, to hand over his piggy bank and say, "I want to give this away, Dad. I don't want it any more." Ask him whom he wants to give it to, and whether he wants to feed the birds or the poor children or give shoes to those people he saw on television, walking through the desert with those packs on their backs, help him to turn his symbolic money into the reality of a bag of birdseed or a few toys for the friends he left behind, whose faces he has forgotten but whose poverty he remembers, or a pair of rubber sandals for some Arab refugee trudging wearily along some endless road, weighted down by the burden once carried by the Wandering Jew.

44

Birthdays

ALL children love birthdays, our Asian children in particular. It is not the presents that attract them so much as
the general festivity of the occasion, the solemn joy of being, for one glorious day, the center of the family, en-
throned on a high chair decorated with flowers and ribbons. You should concentrate as much as possible on the
festive aspects of the day and decorate not only your
child's chair but the house itself, putting out the flag and
dressing the living room with paper streamers and bal-
loons. Squeakers, funny hats, Chinese lanterns, games,
they all serve to enhance the air of festivity, but the high
point of the day will be the cake. Only those who have
actually seen a small Korean child gaze in incredulous
rapture at a birthday cake with four little candles can
fully appreciate how much it means to them—to say
nothing of the parents.

Presents are important only in so far as they contribute

to the glory of the day; in view of his modest standards, it is better, certainly in the beginning, to give your Asian child small inexpensive gifts rather than large and opulent ones. I shall never forget how surprised and even a little disappointed we were when we discovered that our younger daughter on her fourth birthday preferred a box of Band-Aids given as a joke to all the other gifts we had chosen with such care.

But our children not only look forward to their own birthdays with joyous anticipation, they equally enjoy those of other members of the family. On my great day, I am not allowed to get up as early as I usually do; I have to stay in bed and lie there, in the company of the cat and the dog, enjoying a cup of tea prepared by the children, waiting until they have finished their preparations in the dining room. The first surprise is usually a drawing from each child, accompanied by notes (in the case of my younger daughter written in her private Sanskrit) replete with crosses for kisses and circles for hugs. The presents, chosen by them personally, have so far been surprisingly tasteful and practical, such as a little red pillow with the printed legend, "OK, just five minutes" for the chair in my study, a brass spiral in the shape of a reindeer for my mail, a notebook with separate sections for "Laundry," "Milkman" and "Insurance." When, finally, I am allowed in, not only do I find my chair decorated with flowers and colored cutouts, but a special treat on my plate for breakfast, a fried egg or a cheese sandwich grilled to a crisp by my eldest which I doubly enjoy because of the bow on knife and fork and the nest of paper streamers in which my plate is embedded, contributed by my youngest.

Birthdays have become the highlights of our family life, but of late a tradition has been added with which I for one am not too happy. On the eve of a child's birthday, after the queen of the morrow has been put to bed, the whole family gathers in the doorway to wave goodbye and to cry plaintively, "Bye, four-year-old Julie! Bye, darling! Goodbye now, bye, bye . . . !"

The children love it, but aging fathers get into difficulties and have to flee into the garden, overwhelmed by the realization that indeed they will never see this little four-year-old girl again. Of course she will be the same tomorrow, yet she will be someone different, no longer the little child that occasionally woke sobbing from a nightmare and could only be soothed by her Dad taking her into his bed where, her head on his chest and holding on to one of his ears in a childish gesture of security, she would fall asleep listening to his heart. She will no longer draw for his birthday a pink little nude astride a purple monster surrounded by rabbits, pussy-cats and birds with the (dictated) legend, "Jesus with long hair on a dinosaur, at the Easter Bunny's birthday party." She will do all sorts of delightful new things, but by doing them become someone else.

I have no advice to offer for this occasion, no magic balm to ease the pain as you walk the darkened garden and gaze in misery at the glistening stars. All I can say is: do whatever you can to prevent the tradition taking root in your family; whoever thought of it had no little daughters proudly beaming in their cribs as they took leave of one more home port of childhood.

45

Religion

SOME agencies put an unrealistic value on an Asian child's religion as registered in his documents. Especially in the case of children baptized on arrival in Catholic orphanages this is often a stumbling block to adoption by non-Catholic families. The family may not mind, the Mother Superior of the orphanage may not mind, the Catholic hierarchy may not mind, the social worker in the international agency minds and that is the end of that. The largest foundlings' home in New York only recently discontinued its practice of half a century's standing, which was to register all foundlings booked on Monday as Catholics, those on Tuesday as Baptists, the ones on Wednesday as Presbyterians, and so on; the same procedure prevails at this moment in Vietnam. If a foundling happens to be picked up by a Buddhist orphanage he is a Buddhist, if by a Catholic orphanage a Catholic; only if the Quakers or the Mennonites find him is his religion self-consciously listed as "uncertain."

But while it may be, to put it mildly, bizarre to burden innocent children with a church affiliation that may rule out their chances of ever being adopted, to enroll your Asian child on his arrival as a member of your denomination is wise. I know one family—luckily, it's only one—who felt compelled by logic to try to give their child a Buddhist education. Buddhists were hard to come by in the Southern town where they lived, so they ended by proclaiming themselves Buddhists too. Eventually the three of them became Unitarians; they seemed none the worse for their excursion into Buddhism except that they remained vegetarians for a year or so; then an iron-deficiency was diagnosed in the mother, and the father began to worry about cholesterol, so they became fishatarians. By now I expect they have regressed into self-conscious carnivores.

In the years after the war a large number of Korean orphans were brought over by Harry Holt, the Baptist farmer from Oregon, who placed them only with families who declared themselves to have been reborn, recognizing Christ as their personal Saviour. Many adoption agencies and other sophisticated observers thought this to be insufficient basis for a judgment as to the suitability of a family to adopt a child; Harry Holt answered that in his experience practicing Christians were good to children, and that he simply did not have the staff or the professional knowledge to judge families by any other standards. His own faith had inspired him to save these children in the first place, he said, so he could not see anything wrong with this method of selection. His arguments did not go far with the Establishment; the outraged agencies managed to prevail upon the legislature to enact a law that put a stop to Harry Holt's activities. All this was many years ago; in Saigon I met one of the social workers who had taken an active part in Harry Holt's official censure; when I asked her as a matter of interest whether she had ever inquired as to the success of the adoptions he had arranged, she replied with the calm smile of the true believer, "No. Whatever the outcome, the procedure was wrong." As she too, obviously, based her decision on Faith, I did not pursue the matter further.

At first sight it may seem ludicrous to turn Asian children into fundamental Baptists or to place a yarmulka on the head of an obviously Mongolian boy, but as all religions worthy of the name are based on the love of God and compassion for one's neighbor your child will soon get the point of religion if it expresses itself in practice. If it doesn't, he will receive an early object lesson in lip-service, which will stand him in good stead in his future dealings with society.

So, by all means, send your child to catechism, Torah lessons, Sunday School or revival meetings; but don't be distressed if it takes him a while to sort out in his untrained mind the angels, lambs, Fathers, Sons and doves which have been part of our theological gallery from childhood. My younger daughter, after months of Quaker First-Day School which she attended enthusiastically, asked me at Christmastime whether Jesus slept with His wings inside or outside His pajamas.

Rather than bewailing this failure of indoctrination, we cheered her first expression of religious practice. When they arrived in our family, our children were congenitally incapable of sharing anything at all; after a few months our elder daughter suddenly gave a whole set of dolls to her sister with the words, "That's what Teacher Louise says Jesus wants me to do." We welcomed her generosity, however dourly executed, as a sign that the teachings of Jesus had begun to make sense to her, whether He wore wings, pajamas, both, or neither.

46

Travel

THERE is no better way of expediting the adjustment of
your child than some judicious travel together at the
right moment.

You should stay put for at least a few months after the
arrival of your new son or daughter from Asia; in those
early stages what the child needs above all is a sense of
permanency. But there will come a point, which can be
determined by some unmistakable symptoms, when it
will be an excellent idea for you to go on a short trip
together, preferably by air, to a place that is unfamiliar
to you too. There is nothing more effective in bringing
about a feeling of relaxation and relief than being strangers together in an unfamiliar world.

The symptom indicating that this moment has come is
a sudden increase in your child's references to people he
left behind in that other, rapidly receding world across
the ocean. The airplane in which he made the fateful

crossing, the link between the old world and the new, will be mentioned in connection with everything that once made up his world; some children even use the word to distinguish between here and there, now and then. They refer to their natural mother as "my airplane Mummy," their childhood home as "my airplane house"; the airplane will increasingly serve as a symbol of the great divide.

It is in the interest of the child and yourself that, before irritation sets in every time he mentions his blasted airplane Mummy again, you help him erase that stark borderline between his two worlds. The simplest way to do this is to go on a vacation—be it only for a long week end—and to travel by plane. The moment the child has flown there and back, the legendary bird that carried him from Earth to Mars no longer has a monopoly; two airplane rides will render obsolete the definition "airplane Mummy"; eventually his references to her will stop.

At first sight it may seem cruel to deprive a child of the comfort of his childhood memories; but in his case the clinging to the people in his past is part of his neurotic resistance to his own yearning for security, it is again the lone wolf's fear of emotional involvement. To help him combat this fear by gently and unobtrusively dissolving the harsh grip of his memories is neither a betrayal nor an unsavory device to bind him closer to you. His only hope for adjustment and emotional balance is to turn away from the past, to find his identity in the present and in his relationship with you. For you to become his real father and mother is not to rob him of something, but to enable him to resume the process of growth and self-realization that should be a child's sole concern.

Apart from this, you will find that to travel with your new child is a surprisingly gay and enchanting experience. He may have entered the rambunctious and disobedient stage at home; the moment you confront together the challenge of unfamiliar surroundings you will, maybe for the first time, have the exhilarating sense of being a true family. His table manners, which have deteriorated so disastrously after those first proud weeks, will return in all their impressive, slightly inhuman precision; he will magically lose his revulsion from vegetables or milk; instead of insisting with the narrow-minded chauvinism of childhood on hamburger or hot dog, he will gamely tackle shish-kabab, Bircher Muesli and Sole Amandine. Instead of the exhausting bedtime battle which has come to resemble the roping of a calf, he will meekly settle down in the big empty bed in the motel room; if the bed is equipped with the baroque invention called Magic Fingers, put the quarter ransom in the slot and treat him to five minutes of teeth-chattering St. Vitus' Dance, supposed to unwind wound-up businessmen. You will be rewarded with such astonished delight that it will seem worth all the quarters in your wife's pocketbook.

You can safely go for a walk around the block after putting him to bed; the fact that you are all strangers here together tends to reassure him that you will be back, something he doubted vociferously at home whenever you dared to sneak out for an evening at the movies. He may even be asleep when you come back, though your stroll has probably been rather short; he will sleep without dreams, all alone in that enormous double bed. When, the next morning, the three of you get together under one blanket to watch TV, you will bless National

Airlines, Howard Johnson, the man who invented Magic Fingers and Captain Kangaroo. For, together and in combination, they have given you a son.

47

"How Well You Handle Them!"

ANY day now, you will hear people who observe your family in restaurant, church or the home of friends say to you, "How well you handle them!" The first time you hear it you may not be able to hide your startled surprise, but you will soon get used to it and, like all of us, acquire the appropriate modest look and warm little phrase, "Thank you." You will be the only ones aware of the patent insincerity of your reaction, unless you happen to meet another set of parents of Asian children; but they can be counted upon not to give away your guilty secret.

As a father, it won't take you long to discover that rather than your handling them, they are handling you with the same ease with which little boys in India handle the elephants on whose necks they ride, steering them by tweaking their ears.

The first time this notion dawned on me was shortly after our daughters arrived. Our five-year-old, after a week of exemplary behavior and ego-building obedience, started to rebel. We were in the bedroom, I had brought in the morning tea, the girls were having breakfast at a doll's table, seated on doll's chairs beside the bed. The older tike upset her milk and coughed with a mouth full of dry cereal; she was asked to get some paper towels from the bathroom and mop it up. It was then she showed the first sullen rebelliousness that we were to come to know so well. I ordered her to proceed to the bathroom on the double in the tone and with the volume that once, or so I flattered myself, made whole ship's crews tremble. She slunk to the bathroom with buttock-protecting slowness; Marjorie lay rigid and wordless; I sat in my chair, breathing through the nose in leonine wrath; suddenly our three-year-old got up from her doll's chair, came toward me and with a little finger the size of a matchstick playfully stroked my nose. It was a deed of such courage and feminine subtlety that she left me agape with outrage and adoration.

I was destined to feel, on many future occasions, exactly this mixture of emotions. It may be rash to confess this in writing, but my younger daughter can wind me around that little finger any time she cares to, whatever transgression she may have committed. Many fathers of little girls may be similarly enslaved, but I suspect that little Korean girls are experts at this form of lion-taming. Like all women from countries where the male rules the roost, they have the magic power of making our breeches drop at the crest of our strutting self-confidence.

This may give us a feeling of unmanly spinelessness, but I cannot see how it can be avoided, once we have committed the irrevocable act and brought into our home a Trojan horse filled with giggling little girls. As a consolation, I can assure you that only other fathers of Asian daughters will know that, rather than your handling them well, they handle you to perfection. Even your wife won't know. Mine doesn't.

48

Guilt

THERE are many pitfalls for parents bringing up children; in our particular case as adoptive parents of Asian children there is one that may warrant singling out. It is our feeling of guilt.

Mothers are especially prone to this danger. The form it takes is insidious; it is the result of a chain of events rather than a single occurrence. Outwardly, the first six months will have seemed to be the critical ones. Although you may at times have had the feeling that you were making a bad job of it, you will have risen to the occasion. Few mothers fail during the first half year because they do not relax sufficiently to give the subtle adversary, their feeling of guilt, a chance to sneak up on them. It is when you begin to breathe a little easier, when at last your relationship with your child seems to be settling down and you have settled down yourself in the role of a wise, firm but understanding parent, that the critical period begins.

If you pause for a moment to size up your situation, you will admit that after six months of virtually total devotion to another person something in you must begin to give out, whether it be patience, vitality, or sheer physical strength; as with every strenuous effort, reaction sets in once you have succeeded.

In our case, especially in that of the women, reaction begins by showing itself almost imperceptibly. You may begin to sleep badly; simple daily tasks that during the past six months you have done virtually automatically will loom as unsurmountable mountains of drudgery, particularly in the morning. For the first time you will look into the future without the rosy spectacles of elation and all you will be able to see is an endless row of pre-dawn risings, tense breakfasts, dreary washing-ups, unmade beds, solitary lunches from the refrigerator eaten standing up at the kitchen counter, a dreary series of unrewarding dinners to be cooked. You do your work as you always did, but you suddenly realize that it doesn't leave you any time to sit down, especially not lately, as if there were more of it than ever before. There isn't, only you have been doing the usual things just a little slower of late, which, after the odd minute here and the odd two minutes there have accumulated, does indeed leave you little time to sit down and relax the way you used to.

While during all these months you have been amazed at your effortless self-control and reassuring maturity, all of a sudden you over-react distressingly to even the smallest provocation. Peccadilloes like his dropping one shoe in the sitting room and the other in the bathroom, or using your Scotch tape without asking, or daydreaming over breakfast, things which in the past did not warrant more than a casual reprimand, suddenly trigger outbursts of trembling rage, leaving you shaking, bewildered and frightened. What on earth has got into you, all of a sudden? Can this be the true, hidden you? Is this what has been buried all this time underneath the charming, easygoing, sensitive person you have always taken yourself to be? Never mind how low your estimate of yourself has been thus far, suddenly you will discover that it has not been low enough.

This immoderate self-condemnation, even more than your immoderate reactions, is a sure sign that you are suffering from a loss of perspective. It all stands to reason: first, there was the exertion of those months when you consistently rose above yourself and coped with the unknown and the unexpected calmly, intelligently and with a healthy sense of humor. As a result, your child now has settled down and is beginning to show the first signs of inner security. These signs, sadly enough, appear to indicate the reverse: instead of becoming more warmly disposed toward you, he has become naughty, obstreperous and beset by defiant, sullen moods. He slouches off to school in a foul mood, after you have yelled at him for being late or for playing with his food and finally spanked him into the schoolbus in blind exasperation. He leaves you behind in the hollow, empty house with the remnants of his breakfast, the beds unmade, his room a shambles and last night's dishes still in the sink. You start out by feeling hurt and indignant, but around midday you will be stricken by the most abject, harrowing, self-indulgent feeling of guilt. How could you, of all people, react so violently, be so beastly to the poor little mite, who must have known so much violence in his short, unhappy life? What demon possessed you to slap those tiny buttocks that must have been slammed so cruelly by brutish people, virtually from the moment of his birth?

It is incontestable that his childhood was neither peaceable nor serene, but to think of him in these terms at this moment is nonsense. He has been naughty and he knows it, but just as you could not help over-reacting to his naughtiness, he could not help over-reacting to your irritation. It is as simple as that, but it will not present itself to you in those innocent terms when you stand there, gazing disconsolately at the contents of your refrigerator at lunchtime, faced with the dreary choice between cheese, crackers and Coke, or yogurt and an apple, or nothing. Chances are that you will decide on nothing, because as a consequence of feeling guilty for having abused the frail, insecure little waif you will want to punish yourself. To fast at this particular moment is about the silliest thing you could do, but the chain reaction of cause and effect is now happily rolling along; the next phase is that when the child comes home you'll want to make it up to him. You'll be more effusive, more loving, more patient, more generous, more abjectly penitent than ever before and thereby thoroughly alarming. His reaction will be one of wariness and cautious appraisal, which can only be done by taking emotional distance. To you this will appear as coldness, a continuation of his earlier sullenness, and at the first pretext, however slender, you will give him a walloping compared to which the spanking of this morning will seem like a dress rehearsal.

Why do you react so violently this time? Because

your kindness, sweetness, generosity and love were not directed at him alone, but as much if not more so at yourself as an expiation of the guilt that has been gnawing at you ever since morning. His apparent coldness will, emotionally, take on the tragic importance of a sacrifice being rejected. The first sacrifice turned down in the Bible was Cain's and you react in the same manner, though fortunately to a lesser degree.

This situation, once it occurs, is not only self-perpetuating but will multiply, like the feedback in a microphone, until the whole thing turns into a shriek. So, be wise: although it may present to you at this point seemingly insurmountable complications, get away for a while, in the company of your husband. Take a week or ten days off; if he has to work, go to a motel on the other side of town. When you come back from that vacation the whole thing will have taken on the unreal aspect of a bad dream.

Chances are that you'll dream again, but for the time being you will be rested and relaxed and able to take up your life confidently, with a sense of fulfillment. For you have taken another hurdle, the worst one so far; no one will ever know how close you came to what jockeys call "a cropper."

Had you spotted your own symptoms in time and acted upon them promptly, you yourself might never have known either.

49

Absence

WHAT about the child, when you go on that vacation?

Whereas during the first weeks after his arrival he was afraid of many things, once he settled down and began to take root his one overriding fear, sometimes dormant, never absent, will be that you will ultimately abandon him in your turn as his own parents did. Without exaggerating its importance, you must realize that this fear will never be allayed entirely; the best you can hope for is that eventually he will be able to live with it and recognize it for what it is: a scar of the soul, a small cross he will have to carry for the rest of his life.

There are a few things you, as his mother, can do to make it easier for him to attain that ultimate inner balance. For one thing, you must, for at least half a year after his arrival, renounce that greatest treat of parenthood now coming your way: a week's honeymoon in the sun or in a motel in the rain, it doesn't matter as long as it is *away*. The second thing is that when you do go you must make sure that he realizes your absence is temporary and has nothing to do with him, in the sense that he is not to blame for it. He will otherwise instantly assume that you are running away in revulsion from the monster of depravity you have finally discovered him to be and that you will never come back if you can help it. Explain to him that his father and you need a week together because you are tired and haven't had a vacation for over a year, that not only he and the other children in the family have their rightful demands but you as parents do too. Find someone he knows and trusts to replace you during your absence, discuss your plans openly and, once you have decided where you are going, let him know exactly where you will be. The night before you leave, take some extra time, sitting on the edge of his bed before turning out the light, to assure him that you love him and are looking forward to coming back to him and that you are going away for a measly seven sleepies, which he can tick off on his hands without using up all his fingers. He may not seem to understand half of what you are saying, but the fact that you tell him without subterfuge will be in itself reassuring.

Other than this, you cannot help his adjustment to your absence. You can call him by telephone once a day and send him frequent picture postcards but, rather than helping him, it is part of your effort to convince yourself that this was a wonderful idea. You will go on pretending it was until, at long last, you come running up the driveway, breathless and shaky, your eyes filling with idiotic tears when you hear that shriek of sheer joy which nothing can equal—"Mummy!"—and press the monster, laughing and crying, against your pelican's breast.

50

What If It Fails?

Not all adoptions, interracial or otherwise, work out. There are cases where after a while, despite all good intentions and high hopes, adoptive parents are forced to the conclusion that they cannot go through with it. This is why, in most states, the law imposes a probation period of six months before the legal adoption.

Let me reassure you, to start with, that failure is rare. In the case of one agency in the United States, out of four thousand adoptions of Korean children less than fifty failed during the first six months and three thereafter; all of the new placements were successful. But there is no use denying that there will be cases where, for some reason, the adoption does not work out. Should this happen to you, remember that to fail is human and that no stigma is attached to the family that decides in the interest of the child and of themselves to ask that he be placed elsewhere. Once the adoption has been legalized in the courts, it is a relationship for life; under the law there is no longer any difference between the rights of natural children and those of adopted ones, and replacement becomes much more difficult.

A number of reasons can be considered valid causes for a replacement. To start with, there is, as in some marriages, "incompatibility of character." This will be the case almost uniquely when the child involved is older than four; infants and toddlers, although some psychologists judge that their characters have already been determined at that tender age, do not have personalities sufficiently pronounced to clash with those of their adopted parents. Once the child has become an individual in his own right, usually around the age of four, a conflict of character that could be called "incompatibility" may indeed arise. The older of our two daughters may well have come into conflict with her first adoptive mother on a much deeper level than that of childish rebelliousness alone. As she had had full responsibility for her younger sister in Asia, she may have confronted the usurper in a battle of wills far ahead of her years. Relationships between women are much more instinctive than meets the eye; it is quite possible for a woman of thirty to react to a child of five as if they were contemporaries. When a child has acquired a precocious independence because of her responsibility for a younger sibling, she is prepared to take on almost anybody in battle, with no holds barred. In this case the decision of the mother to ask for a replacement was wise as she obviously was congenitally unable to cope with it; had she tried to struggle on, she would in all probability only have aggravated the situation; and while she might have escaped without permanent emotional damage, the same cannot be said for the child.

This should be your crucial consideration. If a relationship is obviously not working out, the decision to ask for a replacement should be made as soon as possible; every day a child remains in what, to him, is an unhappy home will jeopardize his chances for a future adjustment to another, more congenial family. In the case of our little girls the replacement was made six weeks after their arrival; this period would seem short enough to be virtually harmless, but we found that the emotional damage was already considerable. And no wonder; to sever all ties with all you have ever known and then to head into an alien land is emotionally very difficult; the child tries to cushion this shock in advance by developing an attachment to his future adoptive parents, based on the photographs and the general description provided by the director of the orphanage or reception center. If these idealized creatures, almost entirely figments of the child's imagination, turn out to be hostile and reject him, this is a traumatic experience even for tough, independent, precociously mature children like most of our Asian ones.

So, whatever you do, don't procrastinate; the moment you feel that there may be a basic incompatibility between you and the child, which should be apparent after the first month, do not hesitate to confess this to your social worker, who will be visiting you regularly anyhow. There are a number of understandable reasons why you may hesitate to do so. You probably talked to your neighbors and relatives about the child before he arrived; to announce now that you were unable to cope with the situation is an awkward confession to make. But to make it and maybe incur the disapproval of your peers is not going to mark you for life or warp your personality; in the case of the child these dangers are acute. To damage an impressionable, partly formed personality because you are ashamed to admit defeat would turn your misfortune into guilt.

Let me repeat that the chance of your adoption not working out is, according to the statistics, so small that it becomes negligible; but there is no harm in being prepared for the unlikely eventuality. No child from Asia is congenitally unable to adjust altogether; it may be that he is congenitally unable to adjust to you. Your supreme responsibility toward the young life, the destiny of which you have already so fundamentally changed, is to do everything you can as fast as you can to find for him the family that will be truly his own for the rest of his natural life. What your neighbors and relatives may say is of small importance compared to what you will say to yourself, alone with your thoughts at dead of night.

Three

Family Life

51

The Official Adoption

THIS is the day toward which all your dreams, hopes and fears have been directed. Until this day your child could, in theory at least, still be taken away from you and given to another couple; after this day he will be your own forever and in all respects. It is almost inevitable that a day so important, so momentous, will turn out to be the most dismal anti-climax you have ever experienced.

At first, the measured, almost somnolent pace at which life proceeds in county courthouses all over the world will keep you in unbearable suspense; but gradually it will get the better of you too, suppressing your tension rather than relaxing it, and in the end you will find yourself taking part in the inane little pleasantries your lawyer exchanges with your social worker, who is there to testify that to the best of her knowledge you are as good a set of parents as the child is likely to get. It will begin to seem to you that the whole procedure is intended to debunk and cheapen the occasion, the solemnity of which you barely dared face as you got up in the grayness of the early dawn.

The explanation is that the adoption hearing itself is merely the recording of an accomplished process, the registration of a series of findings by various experts which, combined, have resulted in the state's acceptance of you, John and Mary Jones, as the adoptive parents of the orphan Ho Thi Min, who shall henceforth be known to all men as Sue Ann Jones. Before the day is over, somebody is sure to giggle as if he were the first to realize that your child's name sounds like Ho Chi Minh; someone else can be counted on to say, "You know, she really looks like her mother."

The hearing itself, when finally it comes, will seem in your present emotional condition to be awesomely solemn one moment and depressingly pedestrian the next. Documents will be read aloud by the judge, who obviously has barely set eyes on them before now; your attorney will be referred to as "Esquire" even if she is a woman; the social worker will testify by merely answering "Yes" or "No" to standard questions put by the judge; there are documents to sign in triplicate, there is a fee to be paid outside, and that is it: have a cigar, you just had a baby.

It will all seem desecrated, awkward and infinitely depressing unless, at the beginning of the proceedings in the judge's chamber, you happen to look at your child. At first he will seem to be the only one among those present who is capable of living up to the magnitude of the occasion, conscious of the fact that this morning will, for better or for worse, determine the course of his destiny.

Sadly, his solemn composure rarely lasts. There are children who, guffawing cretinously, start making eyes at the judge in an embarrassing regression to inane babyhood; others will begin to run back and forth in front of the bookcases containing the leather-bound volumes of the jurisprudence of the nation and have to be forcibly restrained; others again will sit quietly looking from one to another with pensive eyes and then proceed to strip the occasion of its last vestige of solemnity with a ringing belch. Few children will remain a credit to their parents throughout the proceedings; it is their way of reacting to a situation the crucial importance of which has been brought home to them by their parents' behavior, even though, outwardly at least, they seem to attach much more importance to the ice cream you have promised them once the whole thing is over.

There you sit, at last, in some ice-cream parlor, drugstore or diner, at the wrong hour, in the wrong mood and with the wrong people for ice cream. To feed a lawyer and a social worker maple-fudge-ripple at eleven o'clock in the morning will seem to you the last irony of fate on this bewildering, utterly disappointing day that should have been radiant with reverence and gratitude. When finally you drive home you will feel as if nothing has happened, nothing at all worth mentioning or remembering.

Only later, maybe much later, will you become aware of the subtle change that took place this day in all three of you: the transition of a dream into reality. And, judging by our own experience, it will be one of the rare instances in your life when reality turns out to be better than the dream.

52

The Moment of Truth

NOBODY can foretell how long it will take, as that depends entirely on the individual child, but there is sure to
come a moment sooner or later when the question that
you have been asking yourself secretly for so long will be
answered: "How does he really feel about us, as parents?"

There are variations of this question, but there is no
parent in this world who, after adopting a child from
Asia, will not eventually wonder how the child now
sharing his fate truly feels about the adoption, the people,
the affection he receives. That last point is at the core of
the question. For a while it will seem that your sincere
fondness for him rolls off him like water off a duck's
back, that he is just a rambunctious little boy who takes
it all for granted and has not really established any emotional tie with you, however tenuous.

The cause for his reluctance to express his true feelings

about you is to be found in his history. After a miserable childhood, so hazardous and deprived that we can never really know what he went through, after maybe a series of changes in environment which all felt to him like rejections, he has learned to hedge his bets. It is difficult anyhow to say what a child feels; children's feelings shift continuously like the shadows of clouds sailing across the prairie, light and dark alternate in constant succession and usually no one will have any idea what it was that brought about a change in mood, so sudden and sometimes so alarming. Hence your anguished questions: Does he really feel at home or is he secretly longing to go back where he came from? Don't psychologists say that a child will forever yearn for his natural parents even if they mistreated him to a point where the law had to intervene? Honestly, how *does* he feel?

When he finally does tell you, he will most likely do so indirectly. Don't expect him to stand up and say, "I am glad you are my parents and I love you." If he does, it will just be the expression of one of those moods of elation that inspire ebullience, one of the shifting moods of childhood. He will tell you when the time comes in a way that is unmistakable, and never mind how long he has been with you or how stoic and realistic you are, he will break your heart.

Our elder daughter is a proud, independent child who on the surface seems reticent, occasionally abrasive. She was, from the beginning, correct and polite, with excellent manners which were somehow a little chilling. She shrank, not demonstratively but unmistakably, from any physical contact; she suffered being hugged and let herself be kissed, but the absence of a response on her part did not encourage these demonstrations of affection. Gradually, as the months went by, she relented; her manners became sloppy, which was a comfort, and she began to have gratifying moments of mischief. But as to expressing any feelings about her new home, her new parents? This was her secret; and as even so insubstantial an abstraction as a secret gives a sense of independence to its bearer, we did not press her for an answer.

A few days after Thanksgiving we went to our first Parents' Night. The work of the pupils was to be on display in the classrooms and the teachers available for comment. We went first to kindergarten, where our younger daughter exhibited a surrealist vision of a ghost-like creature without arms or legs, like a huge staring newt, slinking through what seemed to be algae; the catalogue listed it as "Julia de Hartog: Mummy singing with long hair." We were shown her first efforts at writing, most of which seemed to run backward; we were told by the teacher that she was a quiet, reserved child who only recently had finally begun to join in a little with the others. It was a surprising revelation, as at home she started talking first thing in the morning and could only be silenced at night by covering her face with a pillow.

In the classroom of the first grade there were drawings of Indians and Pilgrim fathers on display; Eva de Hartog had done very well and we looked at her achievements with pride. Then my eye fell on a large sheet of paper on the wall, full of childish writing. At the top of the page an adult, obviously the teacher, had written in model letters: "I thank you for:" followed by the children's responses. Each child had one line; the first one said, "I thank God for clothes;" then a little girl thanked God for flowers; a little boy, with male realism, thanked God for good food; an apple-polisher thanked God for schools; a poor speller had contributed, "A thank you Gad fer a baby Nancy" and a hypochondriac, "I thank God for my docter." Then, suddenly, among the children's playful messages to God thanking Him for clothes, flowers, food and sunshine, there was one neatly written, properly spaced line that ran, "I thank you God for Parents. Eva."

She had managed to tell us at last.

53

Learning

MOST Asian children have a different attitude toward the acquisition of knowledge than their American contemporaries. The key word of their childhood has been menace: at home everything seemed bent on beating them down, the outside world seemed bent on eradicating them from the face of the earth altogether. The anguish of the struggle for survival that has been their lot expresses itself in the passionate determination with which they set out to harvest knowledge the moment they enter school. To learn, to understand, to acquire knowledge meant, in that other world, to grasp a lifeline leading out of the abyss. Whether they come from Vietnam or Korea, they have from the dawn of their consciousness onward fought like tigers in order to survive; what made them survive was to a large extent sheer physical robustness, but they also emerged victorious over their sad little brothers and sisters owing to their innate intelligence, inventiveness and awareness of others. As in any catastrophe that has befallen mankind in the past, those who survived did so by their wits.

You will find that most of our children are not only intelligent, but convinced of the utter seriousness of learning. A "play" school not only fails to amuse them, it fills them with a deep sense of alarm. A few days after she arrived, our elder daughter was sent to a highly reputable kindergarten where, in accordance with the latest educational findings, all aspects of a child's personality were stimulated except his mind. Children were encouraged to draw, play, build, tend to animals, grow living things in a little garden all their own, but they were not allowed to try to read or write. The effect upon our daughter was bewildering to us; she came home from school scowling, covered with mud from top to toe; when asked if she had had a nice day at school she made an ugly face and expressed disgust so graphically that it failed to be endearing. An experienced and irreverent mother of three Korean orphans in our neighborhood, who had observed her at play for a while and listened to reports about her from her own children, revealed to us what the trouble was: the child was not only bored at school because her mind was out of bounds, she was scared stiff that she had been intentionally condemned to ignorance. In Korea, she had come to identify the fact of being admitted there with privilege and good fortune; to find herself finally inside the sacred walls and then to be confined to finger-painting, expressive dancing and playing leap-frog in the garden was a terrifying experience.

Now she is in first grade in a school which, by modern standards, is behind the times. She competes grimly in

reading and writing with children born to the English
language, most of whom have had a year of preparation
in kindergarten. The fact that she is among the top three
of her class is not so amazing, for she is an intelligent and
inquisitive child; what is amazing and humbling is her innate respect for knowledge, her sense of pride and solemn joy whenever she manages to spell a word right or
to decipher an enigmatic phrase as it drifts by when we
drive through town in our car: "Delayed green," "Home
of the Whopper," "Get Right with God." The most
moving aspect of her diligence—never hinted at, let
alone acknowledged—is that by spelling "Savings and
Loan" or deciphering "Laundry" she feels she makes us
proud to be her parents.

There is a danger in this that we should recognize.
Competitiveness has become so much a part of American
life that grading at school now starts in first grade. It introduces into scholastic competition an emotional element that may result in deep distress at the slightest failure to excel in class. This is regrettable, but we will have
to learn to live with it, I suppose, as we are invited to
learn to live with lipstick at ten and a bra at the first timid
swelling of the twelve-year-old chest. We may be able to
hold out on the lipstick and the bra, we cannot reverse
the trend of premature competition in the classroom. As
this represents a real danger to our children in particular,
you should explain it to the teacher; if she is an understanding woman, she will, although she cannot fly in the
face of progress, be able to take some of the sting out of
the vicious competition grafted upon childhood by the
introduction of grading in the cradle.

She had better do something, or your child will become inexplicably surly, rude, abrasive at the slightest set-back; he will throw down his books on leaving the school-bus at the end of the day, start pushing his food around on his plate and maybe regress miserably to wetting his bed at night. You on your part can help him by playing down your praise at scholastic triumphs, thereby diminishing his distress at failure. Praise instead his triumphs in a field where competition is beneficial: the field of kindness, consideration and generosity. If you can make him believe that you really value an act of kindness toward his brother more than the A with a Star he garnered by writing without a blot, you will have made the lives of all of you easier and scored a small victory for peace on earth and goodwill toward men.

54

Memories

THERE are two schools of thought on how to handle the memories of our Asian children. Some people advise us to discourage them, not by rejecting them but by remaining noncommittal and changing the subject as soon as possible. They believe that, as a result of this treatment, the child will soon forget his past and adjust more readily to his present circumstances and surroundings. Others feel that, effective as this treatment may appear to be, it does not help the child forget his past but serves to make him aware, with the almost extrasensory perception children have in these situations, that his new parents do not approve of his memories and do not want to hear them. The result will be, according to this school of thought, that the memories are driven underground tinged with a feeling of tabu, which means mental anguish.

Personally, I am inclined to listen to my children's reminiscences, whenever they happen to come out, with

interest and attention. Something may be said for not so-
liciting these memories, but it seems obvious to me that
when a child feels the need to talk about them he should
be allowed to do so until his need is satisfied. I am the
more inclined to react like this because I think that none
of us can be quite sure of our motivations for rejecting
these memories. We may sincerely believe that we discourage our children for their own good, to help them
adjust more readily; judging by myself there exists,
mixed with this laudable purpose, a certain amount of
healthy irritation on our part at the discovery that, despite our unstinting efforts, we have been unable to erase
from our children's minds the memories of that other
home and those other parents who either abandoned
them or gave them up for adoption and thereby forfeited
the right to be remembered as such.

As time goes by, you will discover that the child's
memories, if you allow them to come to the surface, will
undergo a subtle change. To start with, there will be no
memories at all, at least not that you can detect. If he arrives at an articulate age he will first have to learn a new
language; memories, being abstractions, are last on the
list of priorities when it comes to vocal communication.
After a while, as he becomes more adept at articulation,
he will tell you that certain things remind him of Korea
or Vietnam, or that in Korea or Vietnam he used to do
things differently. In a previous chapter I mentioned the
next stage, when his memories become tinged with wish-
ful thinking and the mud hut turns into a suburban bun-
galow, the rags into a costly costume and his parents into
wealthy ancestors. Yet, underlying it all, there will remain an accurate and, in childish terms, realistic set of

memories, especially in connection with siblings. If the child has a brother or a sister who remained behind he will become more and more articulate about him or her as time goes by. When he hears that people in the neighborhood are going to Asia, or simply somewhere far away, he may sidle up to them to ask if it wouldn't be possible for them to collect his brother so that the boy might join him in his new family. But time and growth and the lengthening record of new impressions will inexorably make the memories of brother or sister recede until the moment comes—to me a moment of tragedy—when the child finds for the first time that he can no longer remember their names. To witness this, to see your child sit there, trying desperately to remember, ultimately realizing that he has forgotten the name of the dearly beloved for whom he grieved so much, is a heartbreaking experience. If you can help him remember, by all means do so; his anguish will be so obvious, his sorrow so sincere that you will want to help him anyhow. But, as psychoanalysis discovered, we are inclined to forget what we don't want to remember, so chances are that you won't be able to help him out.

Older and more experienced parents whose adopted Asian children have reached adolescence and maturity have told me that ultimately these memories will come back, as they do in most of us. The older we get, the clearer the memories of our childhood become until at the very end we will, theoretically at least, be able to remember impressions received in the cradle. If this is indeed a fact, then we are the keepers of our children's childhood memories in their behalf. The time will come when your son will want to know who he is, where he came from, who his parents were, where he lived, what he was like when he was a little boy; if he has told you, you may be able to remember all this for him; when he starts to put these questions it means that he has forgotten the details himself. There can be no doubt that emotional balance in adolescence is achieved in proportion to self-identification; your refreshing his memory for him may be a significant help to him in the difficult and hazardous trial ahead.

So, recognize your disappointment at the discovery that you have been unable to dazzle him out of all memories of his past, and let him talk about that alien land and those alien people whenever he feels like it. For all you know, he may, by this circuitous route, be trying to tell you who he is, especially if he feels with his unerring intuition in these matters that you are in need of this information to make your relationship with him a more realistic one. Your wife may have no difficulty conforming to the idealized concept you have of her sterling character, but the worst you can do to a child beset by insecurity is to idealize him, to see him other than he knows himself to be. It is always safer to accept without comment a child's concept of himself than to tell him, from the throne of your more sophisticated powers of observation, that he is in error and that the naughty Nguyen Xuan Phong he remembers bears no resemblance to the virtuous little American he is now impersonating.

Potentially the most dangerous psychological syndrome from which these children suffer is that they will indeed, for a considerable time, live in the uneasy conviction that they are now impersonating someone else. It is the inevitable outcome of that radical transition from one identity to another; vocalizing memories of Nguyen Xuan Phong is part of the child's desperate and all-important struggle to give body and guts to the phantom called Johnny.

55

Family Traits

As in all children, you will eventually begin to discover family traits in your Asian child. The eerie part will be that the traits are yours.

This may sound fantastic to you, yet it has been not only our own experience but that of many other adoptive parents. In our case the experience was especially poignant because our younger adopted daughter takes after me much more strikingly than any one of my four natural children. It is not that she simply copies my mannerisms and idiosyncrasies; whether I like it or not and whether it makes sense or not, she is clearly developing personality traits of her own that no child, however adept at copying could ever hope to imitate. She is bull-headed, domineering, opinionated, yet with a sly mischievous humor that is positively alarming in a four-year-old. Her imagination, which as an Oriental import should at least have something exotic about it, runs in exactly the same patterns as mine. All four-year-olds are born storytellers; this is the age when the human imagination is at its most florid and unrestrained. But why is it that nobody else can make head or tail of her stories and that to me they make eminent sense, while I find myself stumped by the fantasies of other children of her age who make me the recipient of the latest installment of their monster, flower, or pussy-cat series?

Maybe it will all go away, I tell myself. But there is the testimony of other parents—not all of them, but a large enough number to make me conclude that many children from half a world away feel, think, react and decide in a way so much like their adoptive father's or mother's that no one can fail to notice the similarity.

Why? What is the mysterious power that makes the budding personality of a child, cast adrift before its individuality was formed, pattern itself after the personality of a total stranger, denizen of an alien world, with whom it has no other relationship than that of two ships in the solitude of the ocean which decide to sail in convoy for a while?

It serves as a reminder that the relationship between parents and children, natural or adopted, is not formed on the surface but that the most essential part of it takes place deep below the threshold of consciousness. Here we touch upon an ancient mystery that has fascinated man ever since he became aware of these matters; there was even a time when it became the subject of a political controversy. It started as an academic battle between the proponents of heredity as the determining factor in the forming of the human personality and those who proclaimed that factor to be environment. The debate became part of the catastrophic clash of the masses when Communism appropriated the theory of environment and aristocratic capitalism clung to heredity.

The heat of the battle has dimmed, the clash of scientific opinions turned political has become a quaint anecdote of history. On the whole, those whose profession it is to study human behavior seem now to tend toward the conclusion that environment and heredity are equally important in their effect on the human personality as it is formed, environment through the establishment of the values and standards that will guide conduct, heredity through providing the basic emotional material. We, from our small individual outposts in the terra incognita of the human personality and its origins, may have a small contribution to make to this discussion. Our experiences with our Asian children can best be summed up as follows: while they undoubtedly arrive with traits and characteristics that have been determined by heredity, their new environment determines whether those traits and characteristics will turn into positive or negative ones.

A vivid imagination, for instance, undoubtedly inherited, which manifests itself originally as mendacity because of the demands of the environment in which the child grew up, can become creative and turn him into a novelist rather than a liar, a helper of his fellow men rather than an exploiter of their weaknesses. This is our responsibility as adoptive parents toward our Asian children. Each of them arrives with his own unique potentiality; it is up to us, to a more decisive degree than we may have foreseen, whether that potentiality will turn into a gift or a curse.

How do we go about this awesome task? I cannot pretend that I have any valid advice to offer. I am an amateur myself, stumbling from compromise to improvisation as best I can, my fingers crossed behind my back. The only thing I can say with some certainty is that no sermon or lesson will have any lasting effect unless it comments on an example given without premeditation. My parents held forth at my brother and myself with millions of words of which I do not remember a single one—they just went in one ear and out the other without provoking any activity between the two. But I remember the smallest detail of my parents' behavior, especially those in painful contrast with their teaching. Both my parents were sincere, generous people whose darkest traits were harmless exuberance in the case of my father and bright-eyed canniness in the case of my mother. I say this without condescension, in the hope that, when my time comes to be scrutinized by my offspring, my own darkest traits, which to me seem to foreclose the very possibility of salvation, may appear as harmless and innocent to them as the sins of my parents do to me.

But all this is merely an aging man's bleak speculation. What it seems to boil down to is that, for the sake of the future character of the children entrusted to our care, we should be as modest as possible in our moral precepts and as consistent as possible in their application.

56

"*They Call Me Chinese*"

Soon the day will come when your child, whether from Vietnam or Korea, will come home from school indignant and tell you that some classmate, aged five, with the cretinous insistence of a drunk, goes on calling him "Chinese."

In itself this is nothing to get excited about; chances are that the little Babbitt means no harm but is merely exercising his constitutional right to be a bore. What it means is that you should, sometime soon, make up your mind how you are going to cope with these situations, which are likely to become more frequent as time goes by. Just to ignore them is not a good idea, as your child's very reaction shows that the time has come for you to help him establish his identity. He looks different, he is bound to be asked many times where he comes from and what his nationality is, so it is part of your task to help him answer these questions to the satisfaction of his interlocutors and in a manner that will increase his self-confidence and self-respect rather than disturb him.

If he goes on being disturbed, this you must realize clearly: it will be your fault. Your excuse may be that you have sinned following the advice of experts; it is considered "good adoption practice" to help a child to identify as soon as possible and as completely as possible with the community in which he is destined to spend the rest of his life. Some social workers, especially those connected with the administrative rather than the practical aspects of adoption, may interpret this too rigidly. I was part of a delegation that went to see the Minister of Social Action of the Republic of South Vietnam to try and work out with him a formula by which his government could allow orphaned infants and foundlings to leave the country for adoption overseas without flying in the face of his own stated policy, which was that the government should endeavor to do whatever it could to keep all children in the country, so they might contribute to the reconstruction of the fatherland. Faced with the impossibility of keeping some of these institutionalized children alive, the Minister, a highly educated and sensitive young man, was loath to sacrifice them for a mere principle. He finally came up with a workable solution: orphan infants in danger of their lives might be released for adoption overseas, on condition that they would not be naturalized by their American parents after two years as was customary, but allowed to remain Vietnamese until the age of eighteen, when they could choose for themselves which nationality they preferred. This was the minimal condition on which the Minister could allow dying children to be saved, so it came as a bitter disappointment, to

say the least, when we were told by representatives of an
international social agency involved in these adoptions
that they could not possibly accept the compromise. It
was "contrary to good adoption practice" not to natural-
ize children as soon as possible after their arrival in the
States; to maintain the fiction of their being Vietnamese
while their adoptive parents were American citizens
could not be condoned. The choice between accepting
the Minister's compromise or condemning the children
to death did not seem to them to be the essential one;
their essential choice was between good or bad adoption
practices and they simply could not bring themselves to
consciously subscribe to the latter.

To put your mind at ease: we got at least some of the
children out in the end with the cooperation of another
agency. The fact remains that there may be experts, especially those who deal in paper children only, who will
insist that your child be naturalized at the earliest possible
moment. According to them, the proper answer to the
little bore in the playground who insists that your child is
Chinese is, "I am not Chinese, Jack, I am an American,
like yourself." After this, theoretically at least, Jack is
left speechless and your child has achieved identity.

In practice, Jack will not be satisfied with that answer.
To him an American is a blond, blue-eyed, light-skinned
baseball fan, whereas your child is black-haired, has al-
mond-shaped eyes, an olive skin and receives higher
grades than Jack in all subjects except history. Jack's insistence on your son's being Chinese is not uniquely that
of a fact-finding mission.

But there can be no doubt in my mind or that of any
other adoptive parent that, whatever some theorists may

say, it is wrong to tell your child to stolidly maintain that there is no difference between him and his classmates. Questions as to race cannot be rebuked by the formula "I am an American like yourself." Your child is not an American, at least not by birth; he was born in Asia even if he had an American father; his childhood is firmly rooted in an Asian culture. In the interest of his own sense of identity he must, as soon as he asks for this, be helped to learn as much about his country of origin as he can, be given an idea of its history and national status, and be made to feel that it is up to him to decide to what degree he wants to identify with his motherland.

As a Dutchman, I thought the Minister's compromise had great merit. Coming myself from a small country which does not assume as a matter of course that all aliens residing within its borders aspire to become Dutch citizens, it strikes me as an excellent solution to allow your child the choice at the onset of maturity. Several of my contemporaries, born of Dutch parents in foreign countries, were in a position where they could choose at the age of eighteen whether they wanted to be Dutch or American or English, whatever the case might be. As I remember it, they all chose to be Dutchmen because Holland was the country where they had spent their boyhood and with which they now identified; but rather than the ambiguity being a burden to them during their adolescence, it seemed to fill them with an unjustified pride. We others regarded them with envy; to be able to decide for yourself what you wanted to be seemed to us an enviable privilege.

As to the immediate present: the sensible answer to Jack's insistence that your son is Chinese would be,

"Sorry, I am from Korea." In case it should turn out that the other does not know the difference between China, Korea and Vietnam, there is always baseball to help him recover his bruised ego, without the need to recover as well from the information that his playmate is an American like himself. In view of America's current relationship with Gooks, the Yellow Peril and Charlie, theorists seem to overlook the fact that if a child is to identify with a community, the community must allow him to do so. As soon as the stern social worker in Saigon has prevailed upon her fellow countrymen to accept our children as first-class Americans, I will be the first to hail her theory of instant identification as excellent adoption practice indeed.

57

"May I Stay Overnight?"

DESPITE their everyday appearance of unconcern and adjustment, our children carry within them, so deeply buried that they may not be conscious of it themselves, the live seed of insecurity.

Even after years of happy family life there may be occasions, harrowing and unexpected, when you suddenly realize that, despite everything you have done and despite the time that has gone by since they became members of your family, your Asian children still suspect that one day they will wake up and find you gone. Our younger daughter still asks at times, when I go out in the evening, "You are not coming back, are you, Daddy?" She asks it undramatically, without any outward sign of worry or concern, but she asks it, and the question, God knows, is serious. Nowadays I no longer extend my answer beyond a smiling, "Of course I'll come back"; but in the past I used to kneel beside her and go into a long explanation that we were a family now, and that every time Mummy and Daddy went away we were sure to return. It obviously did not make the slightest impression on that subconscious suspicion, and I have concluded that all we can do is acknowledge it and respect it as part, maybe a permanent one, of her personality.

For the time being, however, you have to take into account quite realistically that every parting, even for the shortest absence, will cause in your child a resurgence of the old fear of being abandoned. Some parents say it will pass with the years; others feel that what passes is the symptoms, not the cause. To live with that fear needs an effort of will and reason on the part of your child which you would influence only negatively by interference. Your child will have to become convinced by the mere fact that after each absence you do indeed return that his fear no longer has any foundation. You can rest assured that he will combat his affliction; there will come a moment when you can conclude that the battle is won and that he can live with it. It is the moment when, for the first time, he asks you, "May I stay overnight with Jimmie?"

Even if you hate the idea, even if you can't stand Jimmie, his mother's home-baked cookies or their slavering dog that covers his pants with snail's trails at every visit, let him go. This is the first time in his life he has overcome his instinctive fear; this time it is he who has decided that there should be an absence during which you may vanish like thieves in the night. He is prepared to risk it, and we will never fully realize the magnitude of that heroic act.

So, send him off with his pajamas and the obligatory

peace offering for Jimmie's family, only don't let it con-
sist of a bag of your wife's homemade cookies or you will
compound your son's courageous sally into the unknown
with an unnecessary complication.

58

"Who Were My Parents?"

UNLIKE other adopted children, your child has never lived with the fiction that you and he were related by birth. If he came to you at an age older than three, he will remember a good deal about his childhood in Asia. These memories, though suppressed for many years, will be cherished with a vengence when his quest for identity begins at the onset of adolescence.

You and your wife's reluctance to go in for any serious research as regards his natural parents is normal, during the first year or so. Not only is your child beset by a feeling of insecurity for quite a while after his arrival; you are too. Instinctively you have bolstered your concept of yourselves as his parents by banishing from your consciousness all awareness of his natural parents. You have known something about them, as this information was part of the first document you set eyes on in which a child was described with an outlandish name in the bland

and impersonal terms of a social worker in his home country. You were interested in the identity of his parents then, as your overriding desire was to get some idea, however sketchy, of his background and possible future characteristics. Yet the moment he arrived in your home your subconscious lowered a fireproof curtain between you, his new parents, and his natural ones. A woman especially needs this mental blocking-out in order to make the frightened and vulnerable child her own. No mother can function with the full richness of her potential love and protectiveness until she has made a child hers alone, excluding all others.

During the first years this is the way it should be. Not only she but the child will want to forget what went before, he will want to identify with her as fully as possible. Necessary as this self-suggestion may be, the fact remains that these children are not our own, that we are not their natural parents and that, like every human being, they will at a given moment in their lives feel the need to know where they came from, who their ancestors were, with which gifts and curses heredity has blessed or burdened them. Any parent who, for whatever psychological need of his own, frustrates that need by neglecting to collect all information on the child's background and ancestry while there is still time will have no excuse when the young adult confronts him. It may undo much of the trust and affection that have been accumulated over the years.

If your child is a foundling, do not rest until you have all the information as to where he was found, when, by whom, what the circumstances were; make sure you get a list of all the belongings that may have been found with him and have these dispatched to you if possible, even if there was nothing but a few rags. Recognize your reluctance to do so for what it is; do not fall into the trap of telling yourself that at the age of discretion he may be ashamed of being a foundling. If he should be ashamed it will have been your doing and you will have a hard time defending it, especially if every Christmas you have prevailed upon him to go down on his knees in front of a little creche in adoration of a child wrapped in a rag like the one he himself was found in. If he was abandoned after the bombardment of a village in Vietnam and picked up by a soldier who delivered him at the nearest orphanage, try to collect every scrap of information that may eventually lead to the discovery of the identity of his parents.

The hardest time is had by the adoptive mothers of children whose natural mothers gave them up for adoption to grant them a better chance in life. In most cases the natural father has either deserted the family or been killed in the war; many an Asian widow comes to the conclusion that if her children were to stay with her they would have nothing to look forward to but a harsh and bitter life which would irrevocably coarsen them and keep them in ignorance and poverty. Seeing these delightful and utterly lovable children, every adoptive mother will realize, even if she does not allow herself to articulate it, the awesome sacrifice of the unknown, uneducated Asian woman. To her, the beneficiary of that sacrifice, the haunting thought of the unknown woman is the most formidable obstacle she will have to overcome before she can fully convince herself of the validity of her own motherhood.

It would be fatuous for me to intrude upon this private process with cheap advice; all I can do is point out that this state of mind is very common, and thereby maybe lessen somewhat the secret, gnawing sense of guilt that inevitably results from this situation. It is too much to ask of any woman involved in the process of becoming the mother of a ready-made child to go about collecting information on her predecessor; this is the responsibility of the father. He has power of attorney for the young adult who, had he been old enough, would have tried himself to establish his origins. If the central question of adolescence— "Who am I?"—appears to the boy to be unanswerable forever because these origins are shrouded in mystery, it will be tragic if he concludes that his adoptive parents connived to keep him in the dark for their own comfort.

That day of reckoning is distant as yet; for the moment, the father is faced with the fact that, although it is a condition for her own motherhood that his wife shall banish from her mind all thought of that other woman who once bore the child under her heart, she will never be able to accept this for the psychological necessity it is. Eventually, when she can face it, she will think of this blotting out as a voluntary act of weakness or moral cowardice, something utterly selfish and despicable that she has done of her own free will. The day will come when she realizes that the realtionship between her and her child is in no way threatened by this secret sharer; it is for this day her husband must prepare, by discreetly gathering the information.

Some agencies in Asia press parents for yearly photographs of their child, to reassure the natural mother that her choice has been a wise one and to encourage others to do the same. At first sight, this seems to be a natural thing to do, a simple act of human kindness. There will be parents, however, who balk at the idea, and they should not hesitate to follow their own impulse in this matter. Some parents simply cannot operate wholeheartedly and naturally if the presence of the distant woman is kept alive in this way, and as it is of supreme importance for the child that his present parents shall be his own in the fullest sense of the word, each couple must think of themselves first before deciding whether to comply with the agency's request. If some feel they can do so, by all means let them do it; those who feel nervous or troubled or emotionally reluctant should banish all feeling of guilt from their minds and firmly turn down the request, without apologies. Our responsibility is toward the child at this juncture; his natural mother gave him up, if for the best of reasons, and she should be considered only if a continued awareness of her is not a hindrance to either parent. Honesty and directness are the greatest assets for successful parenthood; in this instance we should unhesitatingly be ourselves. There are times when to refrain from a noble act takes moral courage; in your case, this may be one of those occasions.

59

"Will I Ever Go Back?"

THIS is another question we may have to answer one day. Our children will always carry the signs of their heritage, and some may be prevented thereby from completely adjusting to our society. The documentation of the results of interracial adoptions, now complete up to the age of maturity proves this to be rarely the case; but what would be the fate of your child should it turn out to be impossible for him to adjust? Will he be facing a life of frustration and insecurity? The answer lies not with society but with the child himself; and to some extent your own attitude and your concept of adoption will predetermine his sense of pride and dignity. We can tell our children until we are black in the face that their being different is a potential blessing, but we will fail to convince them of this unless we sincerely accept that they are ours only in trust, that we have received them in to our homes not to appropriate them as vessels for our love but as individuals entrusted to our care so we may help them realize their potential as fully as possible. We can say these things, we may even believe them, but we may discover when we submit ourselves to honest scrutiny that, deep down, we resent the fact.

We cannot change our own emotions by telling ourselves that they are not nice. All we can do is face them and realize that imperfection is the mark of humanity, and that to do the right thing does not necessarily mean that our souls will be flooded with celestial joy as a reward. Many times in the past have I done the right thing without enthusiasm; quite often, to do so has made me feel victimized and resentful.

What is best for our children? This really is the question. To my mind, there can be no doubt that the best is to leave the option open for the child to choose himself whether he wants to follow the destiny imposed upon him by his race or the mixture of it, or whether he wants to take in his stride the fact of being different and make a place for himself in our society. I feel that we are under the obligation to keep alive in our children, should they express the need for this, the awareness of their origins and of the ties that bind them to Asia. On the brink of maturity they may decide that, having profited by chance or by Divine guidance from a privileged youth compared to that of their contemporaries, they want to plow back into the soil from which they came the benefits of the blessings they received. It is quite conceivable that a Vietnamese boy will eventually return to his motherland as a doctor, a teacher or a social worker; in the case of Korean children of mixed parentage this possibility may at present seem more remote, given the barbaric

attitude toward children of mixed blood which still prevails in that country, but at least among the professions a
reversal of this prejudice is becoming evident. By the time
the children are old enough to contribute their skill or
knowledge to their motherland, the popular attitude may
well have changed fundamentally. It would seem to be
our task to prepare them for that eventuality, so as not to
limit their option.

When the question comes that heads this chapter, we
should be prepared to answer, "Of course, if you want
to," despite the twinge of sadness we experience deep
down inside us at the thought that the plane which once
brought them here and gave us so much happiness may
one day take them back.

Appendices

Appendix A

SOME COMMON OBJECTIONS
TO THESE ADOPTIONS

1: "Adoption is not the solution"

THE first time I heard this one was in Saigon, during the summer of 1967. I had just come back to the hotel, sick to my stomach after visiting my first Vietnamese orphanage, haunted as I entered the lobby by the faces of dying infants in iron cots and by the vision of hundreds of toddlers lying apathetically on the hot concrete of the courtyard in the scorching sun, some masturbating in vacant boredom, one lapping up his own urine to slake his thirst. On my way to the elevator a war correspondent whom I had met the day before invited me for a drink in the bar.

I had to do something to banish those images from my mind; this was as good a diversion as any. I followed him into the bar, crowded with officials and officers; there he introduced me to a man in his early forties, a government social worker whom I shall call Andrew Hopkins. The three of us had a drink together and talked about the war, the sufferings of the civilians, especially the children; soon I found myself telling the two men in terms that must have been fairly emotional what I had seen that afternoon. They listened courteously; when I had finished, the correspondent said, "I can imagine that what you saw must have upset you, but let me tell you that the place you have seen is nothing compared to . . ." and he mentioned an orphanage in another part of the city. "You are upset because you're new here," he added. "Once you have been in Vietnam for a few weeks you'll see things more objectively."

"But I don't want to see the suffering of these children objectively," I protested. "Only by looking at it subjectively can I hope to keep the sense of urgency I'll need if I want to get some of them out."

"How do you mean, 'out'?" Hopkins asked.

I told him that I had come to Vietnam to trace sixty orphans under the age of three, allotted to our Quaker organization by the Vietnamese government after we had found families in the United States prepared to adopt them. I had expected him to be sympathetic to my mission, but he was not. "I'm sorry," he said, "but I'm afraid that what you are proposing is not merely pointless, it's wrong. I think it only fair to warn you that I will feel obliged to do whatever I can to stop you."

"Stop me?" I asked, incredulous. "Why?"

"For the simple reason that adoption is not the solution," he answered.

"The solution to what?"

"To the problem of the displaced and orphaned children of Vietnam," he answered, patiently. "We are trying to do a professional job here against impossible odds. We are in a country with no welfare organization worth speaking of, riddled with corruption and nepotism, where at every turn you find some tollgate or somebody's cousin blocking the road. Our only hope is that we will eventually convince the Vietnamese that our way of dealing with these problems is efficient and humane; to achieve that, we must not compromise our case by permitting private citizens like yourself to pick over the trash heaps, so to speak, and make off with one or two individual kids for adoption, or for special treatment in a hospital in the States, or what have you. You may not believe this, but just this morning I found on my desk a letter in which some headmaster of a school in New England proposes to grant kindergarten scholarships to Vietnamese orphans under the age of five. I ask you! What are the Vietnamese to think of our insistence on proper procedures if we sponsor cockeyed schemes like that? So, much as I sympathize with your motives, for the sake of the children themselves I must prevent you from compromising the proper professional procedures we are trying to establish. Sorry." And he finished his drink.

We sat in the bar for another hour. It was the first time I had encountered that argument, and I tried to reason with him. I knew myself how difficult it was to visualize any of these children as individuals. You never saw one of them alone, they always came in packs: swarming around a tank manned by soldiers distributing candy, shouting "Ho, ho, ho!" at an American sergeant dressed up as Santa Claus, waving little paper flags and singing in high-pitched voices in honor of visiting dignitaries. Even in a hospital bed they were not alone but forced to share it with two others, whether wounded, diseased, or dying; their numbers made it almost impossible to visualize them separately.

I knew this from experience. While still in America, I had found myself talking about "the" Vietnamese orphans and "the" foundlings of mixed parentage until in the end I felt as if I were working not for children of flesh and blood but for swarms of disembodied little ghosts, indistinguishable one from another, countless identical little faces shouting voicelessly in my dreams. The only way to combat the hypnosis of their numbers, Marjorie and I discovered, was by becoming involved with them as persons on an everyday basis; we escaped from the spell of their numbers only after our own children arrived. Here in Vietnam the only people I had met so far who seemed to be able to consider the fate of one isolated child without the guilty feeling that they were meting out preferential treatment were the nuns who looked after the children in the orphanage I had just visited. But even the Mother Superior, who had left her office for an hour to accompany us through the wards, had seemed reluctant to allow one child to be singled out for salvation among the hundreds milling around her, as if she thought it more virtuous to let all of them perish in misery and deprivation than to permit one of them to get away. "Perish" was not too strong a word; the mortality rate of infants under eighteen months in the orphanages of Saigon was horrendous. Sixty doomed infants could be saved in this instance by placing them with American families for permanent adoption; to prevent their leaving the orphanage would literally condemn them to death. Certainly as many of them as possible should be helped, as soon as possible, but if sixty out of half a million were placed for adoption overseas it would neither retard that help by one second nor take anything away from the others. On the contrary: seeing these adopted children in American communities might stir more private citizens in America to support such help, while to the orphanages it would mean sixty mouths less to feed. In my opinion, Andrew Hopkins had no case beyond the abstract maxim that all relief should be directed at the greatest good for the greatest number of people. To sabotage the saving of sixty children on that basis alone seemed indefensible.

But although he was courteous and patient and, once the drinks took effect, even amiable, he remained adamant in his determination to stop me. "Adoption is not the solution," he reiterated, stubbornly.

Maybe the Dubonnet we were drinking was stronger than I remembered, maybe it was the passion of the moment, but I must confess I quoted to him a line from William Blake's *Jerusalem:* "He who would do good to another must do it in minute particulars; general good is the plea of the scoundrel, the hypocrite and the flatterer."

He took it with good grace, there never seemed to be any feeling of personal animosity toward me on his part. I was, to him, simply a well-meaning but dangerous dilettante about to corrupt the professional purity of his planning; he obviously had made a decision of conscience and a man's conscience is not up for revision during the cocktail hour. But at the time I still thought he could be convinced by arguments.

My last argument was, "The child I was looking for this afternoon is called Nguyen Xuan Phong. He is eighteen months old, a foundling, and the American doctor who saw him said that unless he was taken out of the orphanage within a week he would die. How would you feel toward someone who was trying to stop me if the child's name was not Xuan Phong but Andrew Hopkins?"

He smiled, rose to his feet and patted my shoulder. "Jolly good try," he said, then he winked at his friend and left, undaunted. Only later did I realize that I had tried to argue with an article of faith.

Should you encounter this argument yourself, you might as well realize before you start that you will never convince your opponent, not even by pointing out that, according to the theory that aid may only be given on the basis of the greatest good to the greatest number of people, Jesus' miraculous healings were impermissible demonstrations of preferential treatment. It is more than just a philosophical problem: why should one sufferer among the thousand be granted the grace of the Master's attention? Why Lazarus and not another?

We may never know the answer to that question, but at least one answer seems wrong: that for the sake of fairness the miracle shall be undone and its beneficiary thrown back among the sufferers. The reasoning that no man shall be granted the grace of Salvation unless all are saved makes sense only to a computer.

2: *"They can be looked after much better in their own, familiar environment"*

All experts agree that in the long run, a child is infinitely better off, emotionally and psychologically, in the environment of his origin than in another culture where he has no roots, even if the material circumstances there are better. The argument sounds convincing; there can be no doubt that those who use it today are sincerely trying to protect the abandoned and orphaned children of Vietnam. The only thing wrong with their reasoning is that, obviously, they do not know the environment in which these children live.

In most of the orphanages I visited in Vietnam all children under the age of two were kept in iron cots with a plastic webbing or wooden slats in the bottom. This does away with the need for diapers; the child's urine and feces fall on the floor under the cot and can be swilled away by buckets of water thrown at odd intervals. Babies are picked up as little as possible, because to pick them up means to stimulate them to clamor for attention, which would mean more work. As a result they all lie helplessly on their backs, rolling their heads from side to side, and flattening their soft small skulls until they ultimately become pointed. It was by the shape of his head that we came to estimate the time a given child had spent in the orphanage; the first thing that struck me on my return to the United States was the beautiful round heads of the babies and the alertness with which they observed the world around them.

The arrival of a visitor in an orphanage usually means a sudden burst of activity by the native women helpers, called amahs. On one of my visits, when we entered the ward, one of the women squatting against the wall at the far end of a row of cots got to her feet, picked up two babies and carried them to a high dressing chest, where she began to paint the sores on their heads with the standard copper-sulfate solution. I turned away to talk to the Mother Superior, who was accompanying us; suddenly a Vietnamese officer in our party who had been watching the amah gave a startled cry. We looked around and saw that one of the babies had dropped off the chest onto the concrete floor. The amah picked the inert little body up by an arm, carried it back to its cot, dropped it inside and returned to the dressing chest, where she continued to paint the skull of the one who was left. It was not cruelty, not even callousness; the Mother Superior explained apologetically that these women, being Buddhists, considered each individual's life to be the continuation of a previous existence—all that was meted out to a human being in his present incarnation was the outcome of his own actions during that previous existence and should not be interfered with, as it might be part of his redemption. The amah had picked up the babies in the first place only to cater to our foreign attitudes.

I saw, during the rest of that visit, two infants die of no apparent cause but emotional neglect. Every nurse who deals with babies knows that unless children receive a certain amount of sheer physical loving care they will, at a given moment, turn their faces to the wall and die, as if by choice. During the worst of the famine in Holland, in the last winter of the Second World War, the Supreme Command of the German army of occupation allowed two bargeloads of babies less than a year old to leave the city of Amsterdam for hospitals in Friesland across the Zuider Zee, where food was more plentiful and where they would be looked after by a professional staff. The barges sailed in bad weather; one of them was blown off course and ran aground on the beach near a fishing village north of the city. The babies were in a pitiable state of hunger, seasickness and sheer terror; the fishermen of the village waded out to the ship and formed a human chain that passed them to the shore, where they were taken over by the women. That night every woman in the village, young, old, single, married or widowed, had a baby to look after. A few days later the barge was refloated and entered the harbor to take on its load of babies once more. But the women refused to give them up; despite the dire threats from nervous officials, not one child was delivered on the quayside. The barge returned empty to Amsterdam.

In each barge there had been two hundred children; of the ones who ended up in the hospitals across the water, where they were well nourished and looked after by shifts of professional nurses, one quarter died, yet all the babies taken in by the women of the fishing village survived, despite the fact that their rations were far inferior and that there was no professional help available.

There is no substitute for the life-giving comfort and warmth of being hugged, nuzzled and loved by one motherly woman, and there can be no doubt that Vietnamese babies in the same desperate condition would respond as well to this treatment as the kidnapped infants

of Amsterdam did, if only those whose professional duty
it is to safeguard their well-being would close their books
of rules and let them go.

3: *"Why not a child from your own country?"*

The social worker assigned to your case, when she first
visits your home, probably will have this question upper-
most in her mind. But she is unlikely to put it to you, at
least not directly; the people who do are usually ac-
quaintances, even total strangers, who for some reason
react with irritation and hostility to the information that
you are planning to adopt an Asian child.

Is the question a valid one? Objectively speaking, it is;
the social worker will think so, but as it is not her business to berate you, only to pass judgment on your suitability as adoptive parents, she will with a sigh and a
shrug start investigating you, ascribing your preference
for a Korean or Vietnamese child to fashion.

Should you ask yourself this question? There is no
harm in doing so, but I personally do not think there is
any point to it. Even those who do not believe in Divine
guidance must sooner or later come to the conclusion that
there are things in life which should be accepted and not
questioned; useful and sometimes necessary as self-
analysis may be, in basic decisions like this the danger is
that too intense a scrutiny of one's own motives will
bring about doubt, and that doubt will lead to one's aban-
doning the whole idea. As even the most ungenerous social workers agree that it is better to adopt a needy child

from Asia than no child at all, they will not bug you
with the question. But what should your answer to those
others be?

The relationship between you and your future child,
like the relationship between any parent and his offspring, is an emotional one. Only a small part of our identity is revealed within the horizon of our consciousness;
our moods are ruled and our acts steered by currents and
streams beyond the range of our perception. Why did
you fall in love with your wife and not with the girl next
door? Why do you instinctively like one person and just
as instinctively dislike another? We can analyze ourselves
until all our psychological tendons and viscera lie exposed in the unflattering Klieg light of our scrutiny, and
we will know no more about the source of our motivation and the course of our destiny than we knew before.

I believe that in this particular respect you should allow yourselves to be guided by whatever wind it may
have been that carried the notion, like the seed of a dande-
lion, from that unknown field half a world away, across
plains and mountain ranges and the immensity of the
ocean until it alighted in the fertile soil of your inarticulate longing. In the face of that mystery, the question
whether the thought of adopting a child from Asia was
reasonable when it occurred to you is immaterial. You
were moved to reach out to an unknown child in an unknown land; the essence of your humanity demands that
you shall go on reaching out until you can shelter it and
give it life, not that you shall furnish a socially acceptable
motivation for your impulse.

Maybe I have had more than my fair share of this type
of inquisitioner, but the longer our children are with us

the more impatient I feel with people who, from the objectivity of their non-involvement, demand a satisfactory answer to the question as to why I did not adopt a needy child from our own community. After trying for a while to come up with a reasonable reply I at least found a retort. Now, when someone comes drifting toward me at a meeting or a party, glass in hand, to call me to task, I say, "That's a good question. If you feel so strongly about it, why don't you?"

4: "Did you know that they are bought from their mothers?"

The origin of this rumor may be that some agencies in East Asia are in the habit of giving a small donation to an orphanage or reception center after they have placed one of its children for adoption abroad. The sum of money involved never amounts to much, and is certainly not to be classified as "the price for the child." It is more like a symbolic gesture of appreciation to the orphanage, expressing awareness of the circumstance that the children who remain behind are the innocent victims of a caprice of fortune, or of the mysterious ways in which God works His wonders to perform, according to one's personal interpretation. To make a donation of fifty dollars to an orphanage trying to care for seven hundred orphans, in the space for three hundred and on a budget for one hundred, can hardly be classified as a transaction in the slave trade. When I was roaming the nightmarish halls of the orphanages of Vietnam I came to the conclusion that to donate fifty dollars to any one of them would be like giving a peanut to a starving elephant.

Another cause for this rumor may be the laudable practice of one Korean social agency to make an effort at rehabilitating the mother after having placed her child abroad. It does this by giving her a training which may result in her opening a little shop, or by finding some other type of work for her that will save her from having to return to her old, familiar environment.

Although it cannot be substantiated and is clearly a figment of somebody's private demonology, the rumor persists, so it may be more effective to ask the person who brings it up whether, in his opinion, this consideration should decide whether a child should live or not. Suppose at some moment, in some dark corner of the twilight world where these children swarm, some money secretly changed hands in return for a babe in swaddling clothes. If one participant in this transaction is innocent, surely it is the child itself. To refuse him a chance to lead a normal life, or any life at all, as retribution for other people's sins is unacceptable even to those who perpetuate the rumor. Or, at least, they will agree it is.

5: "In this country they would be horribly spoiled"

An elderly lady in a semi-official position, who had been highly vociferous in her objections against "the import of Asian children," was cornered by some of our parents after a meeting and badgered until, flustered and furious, she finally came out with one specific reason for her active opposition. These children, she said, so appealing to look at, would run the grave danger of being spoiled rotten once they got here and thereby become impossible to live with in later life.

To us, at the time, it sounded like a ridiculous argument; we discovered to our surprise that a number of educational experts, while conceding that the lady in question might have exaggerated the danger, sincerely thought she had a point. Our children, they feared, might indeed run the risk of being severely spoiled, with the result she mentioned.

In a sense, they were right. All of us with children from Korea or Vietnam have found ourselves in situations where, in a restaurant, an airport or a supermarket, total strangers come up to our children to say, "Now aren't you a cute little baby? Aren't your Mummy and Daddy lucky people to have two such darling little girlies to call their own?" Mummy and Daddy, case-hardened by now, may wince as they smile; to the children, if the worrying experts are right, this will be acutely harmful. You cannot go on calling an impressionable, brightly intelligent urchin "cute," "darling" or "the sweetest thing I ever set eyes on" without, so it is argued, force-feeding him with flattery until he turns into a mini-megalomaniac, strutting where he used to skip, saying his prayers with pigeon-chested condescension, as if he were ordering a menu from room service rather than humbly approaching his God.

I cannot agree with this somber prognosis. Were we ourselves to indulge in this kind of hyperbole at home it would be a different matter, but to fear that occasional

admirers, mostly elderly, ingenuous and harmless, will in-
flate our child's ego until he has to be clubbed in front of
the mirror seems an exaggeration. On the contrary, although that kind of situation is always icky and awkward to get out of, I welcome the occasional sentimental-
ist who feels he simply has to tell my children how
pretty, cute and clever they are. Although I am at pains
to hide this from my wife, I don't even blanch when
some effusive fan, peek-a-booing among the bolognas or
the rolls of toilet paper in our local supermarket, reminds
my children how lucky they are to have such a darling,
selfless Daddy; for not only have I a high tolerance for
flattery, but my common sense compels me to relate the
episode to our children's past. After they have survived
years of unimaginable deprivation, especially emotionally,
I cannot understand why they should be considered too
fragile and insecure to take some harmless, drooling adu-
lation in their stride. What is more, the reception that
awaits them here is not always so generous and benevo-
lent as we would like to believe. Why we should worry
about their being spoiled by praise while assuming them
to be immune to contempt escapes me.

6: *"They will never be really yours"*

Among the dire warnings you will be given by other
people, this one may impress you most. But to think that
any child, even a natural one, can ever be one's "own" is
asking for trouble at the onset of adolescence, when the
human young awakens to the fact that the people he has

been calling his parents are not only purely incidental to his identity, but complete strangers who, rather than understanding him best, are about the last people in the world to understand him at all. Only after the egotist who flew the coop has reached maturity himself, through marriage and parenthood, will he modify this concept of your relationship—usually about the time he starts doing something about Mother's Day again after a long interval.

In the early years of interracial adoptions it was assumed by social workers that this type of adoption was more hazardous than the normal kind, where a child was selected to resemble as much as possible one or both future parents. Adjustment, it was thought, became easier in direct ratio to the closeness of this resemblance. When practice began to prove that interracial adoptions worked out better on the whole, experts delved assiduously into case histories for the reasons for this discrepancy, and after a while one did emerge: because of the difference in appearance the adoptive parents of an Asian child were unable to hide the fact that he was adopted. This, rather than causing emotional distress in the child and parents as had been assumed, made for a healthy, realistic relationship. The fact that people saw at a glance that the child was adopted ruled out the tragic situation, fairly common at that time, in which a child after having lived for years in the conviction that his parents were his own was suddenly exposed to the traumatic discovery, usually by accident, that he was adopted.

I can tell you, even after so short a time as a year and a half, that my Korean daughters and I are joined by a relationship which is surprisingly deep-rooted and affectionate. I am proud of them, fascinated by their unique individuality and moved by their unselfconscious tenderness. They may not be mine, but I am theirs, without reservation; and to my surprise, for reasons known maybe only to mothers, this turns out to be all I need to feel at peace with the world and grateful to be alive.

And if you think that's mawkish, just you wait.

7: *"You will never love them the way you love your own children"*

At one time I thought I would never find bureaucratic unworldliness expressed more succinctly than in the question, the last on a list of thirty submitted to aliens who desire to become citizens: "Can you read or write?" I have since been forced to transfer my laurels to a questionnaire for prospective adoptive parents composed by a concerned social agency which contains the following item: "You have one child of your own. If both your own child and the one you propose to adopt were to fall into the water at the same moment, which one would you rescue first?"

You will find that this question, once you have allowed it to sink in, will go on haunting you; at first because of its surrealist preposterousness, like the mathematical problems of our schooldays, "Five Chinese eat seven bags of rice, how many bags of rice does each Chinese eat?"; later by the nagging thought that, indeed, the agency may have something there.

Do parents who have children of their own ever love

adopted children as much as they do their own flesh and blood? For a while it may seem to you that the question is not only searching, but valid. Only after you have managed to rid yourself of the spell that the self-confidence of ignorance always manages to throw on one will you awaken to the abysmal stupidity of the concept that love should or can be ladled out, like soup, in equal parts among your dependents with scrupulous impartiality.

Love, if its illusive mystery has to be defined for consumption by a Univac, is an emotion engendered by one person in another which will ultimately result in an unselfishness uncongenial to the human animal. In its sublimated form, so the mystics tell us, it does not even need an individual but can be engendered by all mankind and ultimately by all living things. But even in that rarefied and superhuman form love remains an intensely personal emotion which has nothing to do with duty, sense of responsibility or the desire to give everybody a fair share. If my children could reassure themselves on the subject of my love only by jumping in the water with their hands tied behind their backs and weights attached to their legs, in order to find out whom I would rescue first, they would deserve to drown and the person who composed the questionnaire with them.

But once you have shaken off the questionnaire, the question remains unanswered. It should remain unanswered, but such is human nature that we will go on asking ourselves, in secret, especially during the months before the child arrives, "Will I, when put to the test, give preference to my own flesh and blood, although on the surface my adopted child will share equally in my affection?"

It needs the reality of the human presence before this mad bat of a question can be chased back into the bureaucratic belfry from which it swooped. It needs the actual feel of a little body in your arms, the actual sound of a voice calling you Dad, the actual stumble toward the toilet at dead of night and the patient wait for the tinkle with your knees on the cold floor and a small sleeping head on your shoulder, for you to realize with a feeling of inexpressible relief that the concept of love as a limited fund that has to be doled out in ever smaller portions as the number of claimants increases is nonsense. So you end up by loving one child more than another, or in a different way? The Bible is full of favorite sons. They figure honorably in American presidential elections. Which child expert, family-planner or adoption-plumber can demand that parents sign a document stating they shall love a child they have never set eyes on to the same degree and in the same manner that they love their own offspring whom, at times, they would gladly strangle?

Each new generation of young girls hears it said and reacts to it with a sense of revelation that, in the beginning, a person is in love with the idea of love, not with one particular human being. We parents start by being in love with the idea of a child, until the individual hacks his way through the foliage of our sentimental generalization. Never fear, he will; probably sooner than later. In no time at all he will stop being "the Vietnamese orphan you and your wife adopted," he will stop being orphaned, Vietnamese and adopted in succession, ultimately he will even stop being a child and become himself: unique, irreplaceable, never seen on earth before, never to be seen again, absolute and ultimate entity of mankind.

The moment will come when you look, for the first

time, beyond the mirrors of each other's eyes; if at that moment the person who wrote the questionnaire were to come in and pose his question, you would look at him in astonishment and wonder what life had done to him to make him that way.

Appendix B

THE LAW

In the United States, adoptions are governed by state law. Although there is little difference between them as to limitations imposed, some states, especially Southern ones, rule out the adoption of a child of one race by parents of another. Most legislation does mention religion and the age of the parents, but none of the other restrictions commonly imposed by adoption agencies.

The laws are lenient and likely to promote adoption rather than prevent it; the guidelines imposed by agencies are a different matter. In some extreme cases, socially acceptable physical deformities such as a clubfoot, the lack of one or more fingers, even the wearing of dentures may make a man unfit to be an adoptive father in the opinion of the agency concerned. These guidelines date from the time when the supply of adoptive parents so far exceeded that of adoptable children that a rigorous selection based on certain principles had to be made, unless one decided to draw the name of the winner from a hat. Although, obviously, the fact that a man had a clubfoot or wore dentures did not make him unfit to be a father, when it came to selecting one couple of applicants from among a score a case could be made for an agency's preference for a man with two healthy feet and his own teeth. The survival of these cattle-breeder's distinctions beyond the emergency that justified them is, especially when they are applied to the prospective parents of infants from Korea or Vietnam, an insult to the essence of the calling of social work. Yet, as you may discover, some welfare agencies and a few private ones still adhere to "guidelines" like these.

In any case, the Immigration and Naturalization Service of the Department of Justice will have to rule on the visa granted to the child of your choice. As of this writing, the law still prohibits citizens of the United States from applying for visas for more than two orphans from overseas. This means, in practice, that you will not be able to adopt more than two children from Asia unless (and this is provided by law) the second child of your choice should have a brother or a sister whom you would be willing to adopt. The law limiting the number of foreign children you may sponsor still stands, although its days are numbered. Many legislators and Congressmen consider it arbitrary and immoral.

More detailed questions regarding the law on adoptions you will find answered in *Adopting a Child Today* by Rael Jean Isaac; those regarding the issuance of visas to eligible orphans (now called "immediate relatives") in *Immigration and Nationality Act* issued by the U.S. Government Printing Office.

Appendix C

AGENCIES

ANY agency is as good or as bad, as comfortable or as uncomfortable to deal with as the social workers it employs. I have known private agencies, supposedly committed to the most liberal policies of choice and placement, that were chilling to deal with because of the rigidity of the martinets who manned their desks. On the other hand I have known many a state or local welfare agency where, despite stern policies and forbidding guidelines, any pair of parents would have felt welcome and secure in an atmosphere of understanding and helpfulness. In all intermediary agencies of official or semi-official nature, the personalities of the functionaries are important, but nowhere more so than in an adoption agency. To evaluate the suitability of any given set of parents to adopt a child is a delicate business at best; no amount of rules, guidelines or theories will ever equal in importance the personal empathy between the investigator and her subjects when it comes to this evaluation.

I found most parents of Asian children agreed that if you run into an unsympathetic social worker during your first visit to a welfare agency you should transfer to another agency. Love or loathing at first sight are so important in this situation that it can almost be assumed the initial meeting will determine whether, in the end, the agency will accept you or no. I know of two cases where a family had been investigated by two different agencies; the reports on the family read as if they concerned a different set of people. When asked how they explained this discrepancy between the results of the two home-studies, both families replied that, in the instance of the agency that turned them down, they had felt an instinctive dislike for the social worker assigned to their case and this dislike had obviously been mutual.

There are, of course, certain basic rules which even the most sympathetic social worker cannot disregard so long as they form part of an agency's policy. Certain agencies, especially private ones, will not accept parents over a certain age or will adhere vigorously to the matching of religions; the latter restriction should not worry you unduly although there still are some agencies that stolidly refuse to place a baptized Asian foundling in any but a Roman Catholic family. If the foundling is confined to an orphanage in Vietnam, this means that the power the agency holds extends itself over life and death; normally this power is limited to the granting or not granting of children to families unable to have children of their own. This already is a pretty substantial power for a human being to exercise at his discretion; as in all situations where a person is given power over others, it will irrevocably corrupt unless accompanied by the counterparts, love and compassion. Love for children and compassion for the parents will make the social worker investigating your home an ally and a helper rather than an inquisitor; the bewildering aspect of the problem is that the same social worker may in one case conform to the first description and in another to the latter. It is, indeed, a matter of personal empathy; so if you feel a noticeable element of hostility and suspicion among the three of you during your first visit, don't go on; explore alternative possibilities at once.

The best way to proceed is to start with your local welfare agency; if you find that your case does not receive sympathetic consideration there, write to Welcome House (Box 6, Doylestown, Pennsylvania) if you live in the Eastern half of the United States, or the Holt Adoption Program (Box 95, Creswell, Oregon) if you live in the West. Ask them for the name of an agency in your area that has cooperated with them in the past. There is virtually no region left in the United States that is outside the action radius of an agency familiar with and sympathetic to interracial adoptions. Even if you should live in such a sector, there are alternative solutions which either of the organizations I mentioned will be happy to explore with you.

The need of the orphaned children of Asia is so urgent that you really should try to overcome the reluctance some unfortunate meeting with an unsympathetic social worker may have instilled in you in the past and explore the alternatives. You may never forgive yourself for withholding from some unknown, friendless child the basic right of having parents he can call his own: you.

Jan de Hartog

Jan de Hartog was born in Haarlem, Holland, in 1914, and
ran off to sea at an early age. In 1940, just after the Germans
occupied Holland, his novel *Holland's Glory* was published,
a rollicking story of the Dutch ocean-going tugboats on
which he had served. Although it mentioned neither the war
nor the Germans, it became a symbol of Dutch defiance and
was banned by the Nazis, but not until 300,000 copies had
been sold. In 1943 the author escaped to England.

Since then Mr. de Hartog has sailed many miles and has
written a number of books: *The Lost Sea, The Distant
Shore, A Sailor's Life* (these three are now collected in the
volume titled *The Call of the Sea*), *The Little Ark, The
Spiral Road, The Inspector, Waters of the New World, The
Artist, The Hospital* and *The Captain*.

Mr. de Hartog's name has gained added familiarity through
the popularity of his plays *Skipper Next to God* and *The
Fourposter* (both of which became films, and *The Fourposter* has recently been adapted for the musical stage as *I
Do! I Do!*). Three of his novels have also been made into
films: *The Distant Shore* as *The Key, The Inspector* as
Lisa, and *The Spiral Road*.